BRITISH CHALLENGE

BRITISH CHALLENGE
AT THE 1984 OLYMPICS

PAINTINGS BY
KEVIN WHITNEY
WITH A TEXT BY BRIAN GLANVILLE

Frederick Muller
London

First published in Great Britain in 1984 by Muller, Blond & White Limited, 55/57 Great Ormond Street, London WC1N 3HZ.

Reproduction rights of paintings and drawings copyright © 1984 Muller, Blond & White Limited.
Text copyright © 1984 Muller, Blond & White Limited.

All rights reserved. No part of this publication may be reproduced, stored in a retrieval system, or transmitted, in any form or by any means, electronic, mechanical, photocopying, recording or otherwise, without the prior consent of Muller, Blond & White Limited.

British Library Cataloguing in Publication Data

Whitney, Kevin
    The British Challenge.
    1. Olympic Games – History – Pictorial works
    2. Athletes – Great Britain – Portraits
    I. Title II. Glanville, Brian
    796.4'8'08921   GV721.5

ISBN 0-584-11103-7

Reproduction by Mullis-Morgan Ltd, London.

Typesetting by Input Typesetting Ltd, London.

Printed and bound in the UK by Hazell Watson and Viney Ltd, Aylesbury.

CONTENTS

- 8   Dedication and acknowledgements
- 9   Preface
- 10   **The Challengers**
- 12   **Steve Ovett**
- 16   **Steve Cram**
- 20   **Sebastian Coe**
- 24   Albert Hill, Douglas Lowe, Sydney Wooderson, Roger Bannister, Gordon Pirie, Derek Johnson, Ann Packer
- 33   **Allan Wells**
- 38   Harold Abrahams, Eric Liddell
- 42   **Daley Thompson**
- 46   **Judy Livermore**
- 50   **Fatima Whitbread**
- 52   Lord Burghley, Chris Brasher, Mary Rand, Lynn Davies, David Hemery, Mary Peters
- 64   **Neil Adams**
- 68   **Andrew Morris**
- 70   **Lucinda Green**
- 72   Harry Llewellyn and Foxhunter
- 74   **Beryl Mitchell**
- 78   **Chris Snode**
- 82   **Phil Hubble**
- 84   **Adrian Moorhouse**
- 88   Henry Taylor, Lucy Morton, Judy Grinham, Anita Lonsbrough, David Wilkie, Duncan Goodhew
- 106   **Torvill and Dean**
- 110   Cecilia Colledge, Jeanette Altwegg, John Curry, Robin Cousins
- 116   **The Challengers** – biographical details
- 117   **The Paintings** – details
- 118   Major British Triumphs since 1896

... to Luciana Martinez de la Rosa
'La più bella, la più grande ispirazione'

Kevin Whitney is Sponsored by:
G-P Inveresk Corporation
Budget Rent A Car.

Kevin Whitney would like to thank The British Olympic Association and all respective governing bodies for their co-operation and support. Especially:
Dr D.W.J. Anthony, Education Sub-Committee, B.O.A.
M.J. Blake, Assistant General Secretary, B.O.A.
G.H.J. Nicholson, Appeals Secretary, B.O.A.
C.S. Palmer, OBE, Chairman, B.O.A.
R.W. Palmer, General Secretary, B.O.A.
and all the athletes for inspiration.
Also
Marek Anthony, Personal Assistant
Jasper Morrison
M.C. Parsons, Advertising Manager, G-P Inveresk Corporation
A.C. Brown, Overseas Director, Winsor and Newton, Fine Art Suppliers
J. Stadden, Stadden-Hughes Ltd
N. Walt, Cornelisson and Son, Colourists
Tony Duffy, *All Sport*
Robert McMarn, *All Sport*
Eileen Langsley, *Supersport*
Bob Thomas, *Sports Photography*
Dennis Storer, British Attaché, Los Angeles, U.S.A
Robert Carson
Chelita Salvatori
Jenny Runacre
Pru Walters
Chris Garnham, Photographer
Jass Cameron, Green and Stone Ltd
Holmes Place Health Club, Fulham Road, London

PREFACE

This book is an attempt to picture the present and evoke the past. Seldom has Great Britain sent a more dazzling team to an Olympiad. It includes such gold medal winners as Steve Ovett (800 metres), Seb Coe (1,500 metres), Allan Wells (100 metres) and the world's most spendidly versatile athlete, Daley Thompson, the decathlon champion, as well as the brilliant, more recently emerged talent of Steve Cram, winner of the 1,500 metres event in the Helsinki world championships of 1983. There are also such figures as the elegant rider Lucinda Green; Chris Snode, a fearless diver; Beryl Mitchell, a silver medallist sculler in the World Championships; and Andrew Morris, Britain's best gymnast yet.

Kevin Whitney, a gifted painter who has exhibited internationally, was commissioned as official artist by the British Olympic Association, giving him unrivalled access to the members of the British team and a fine opportunity to exploit a new dimension – to go beyond the photograph to the painting, to try to catch the essence of the performer both in movement and expression.

In his text, Brian Glanville, whose novel *The Olympian* appeared in many countries and was particularly praised in the United States by such gold medallists of the past as Jesse Owens and Don Bragg, has tried to build a bridge between past and present. He has written profiles not only of the outstanding members of the present team, whom Whitney has so vividly depicted, but of most of the British gold medallists of Olympic history.

Thus we have not only Cram, Coe and Ovett but Bannister and Wooderson, not only Wells but Harold Abrahams, who lunged at the tape as Wells does, and was the last Britain to win the 100 metres medal until Wells himself won it, 56 years later. The devout and self sacrificing Eric Liddell, Abrahams' rival in the Olympic games as depicted in the film *Chariots of Fire*, also appears in the book, with challengers from skaters to sprinters, men as well as women – all of them champions.

THE CHALLENGERS

STEVE OVETT

Of the various, brilliant middle-distance runners to emerge in Britain over the last few years, Steve Ovett is probably the most talented and versatile, the most naturally gifted, whether or not he has been the most effective.

A Sussex man, from Brighton, with cropped, receding hair, a sturdy mistrust of the press, and a wayward disposition, he has never cut quite the ideal figure that his rival, Seb Coe, has done. Indeed, he himself has said, 'I represent the brutal, animalistic side of sport. Seb is for the educated, articulate. For most people, it's as simple as that.'

But of course, it's not remotely as simple as that. Ovett has a grim resilience. If you try to jostle, shove or crowd him on the track, he is quite capable of paying you back with interest—even, perhaps, of getting his retaliation in first. But that is only a question of *realpolitik*. If it comes to a pure contest, cleanly run, Ovett at his best is a marvellous match for anybody, a sublime accelerator.

Like Coe, he has produced superb results both at the 800 and 1,500 metres—or mile—distances. In the Moscow Olympics in 1980, Coe was favoured to take the 800-metres title, and the 1,500 seemed a toss-up between them. In the event, it was Ovett who judged a slow 800 metres final much better, and won it, while Coe had the last word in the 1,500 metres.

Like Coe, Ovett had a hard and anticlimactic time of it in 1982 and 1983 with injuries. But, despite his disappointments, he proved his character and vast ability by bouncing back, in August, to regain his world 1,500 metres title on an Italian track. He did, however, later lose a much publicized race in England to Steve Cram.

He has said that things would obviously have been easier for him had Coe never existed, but one wonders. Surely, like the great Swedish milers of the forties,

Haegg and Andersson, they have brought the best out of each other. And now Cram has emphatically begun to bring the best out of both of them.

Although he himself admits that his public image has tended to be a negative one, Ovett is very much an athlete's athlete. Steve Cram has paid tribute to the generous advice Ovett gave him when he was on his way up, and Daley Thompson, a great admirer, was cheering for him in the Moscow Olympics. By the same token, Ovett was very distressed when he and Coe were awarded the MBE, while Thompson and Allan Wells got nothing at all. He thought it 'rather scandalous.'

'Everywhere I go,' he says, 'people come up to me and say, "What about Seb? Do you hate him? What's he really like?" Ridiculous. How do I know what he's like? He lives in Sheffield and I live in Hove and we only meet a couple of times a year.'

Steve Cram, as a youngster, was fascinated by the scene in the Olympic stadium dressing-room before the 1980 1,500 metres final when, in the burning tension, Ovett suddenly went up to Coe. As Ovett recalls the story, the gesture was a frustrated one. 'I tried to discuss things with him once. It was in Moscow, just before the 1,500 metre final. The whole thing had been built up for months: Coe against Ovett, the Big One. I'd already won the 800 metres, so I was pretty relaxed. Anyway, it suddenly hit me that everything was being blown out of proportion, and I looked across the dressing-room and said to him, "All this is for nothing, isn't it? We're just being used." But then I saw how he was, how his whole life at that moment depended on winning the 1,500, and he gave me a look that said, "What the bloody hell are you on about?" So I shut up. It wasn't the time to talk things over. But he knows what I mean, and I dare say he'd agree with me. We were just two ordinary guys, going through hell, even though we knew, deep down, that it was only a sport.'

It was an astonishing perception to bring forward at that moment—something that you might have expected to come from Coe with his middle class background and Loughborough College degrees, rather than from Ovett. All of which shows how easily one can be misled by public images. Athletes are, indeed, widely exploited, however much they are acclaimed, however richly they may be rewarded. But it takes a remarkable man to acknowledge the fact, not only when he is at the very peak of a dazzling career, but within minutes of competing in one of his most important races.

Yet for all the implacable pressures, Ovett admits that he has continued to get pleasure from his running. 'If, you don't enjoy it,' he says, 'you're finished, because you can't take the training. Athletics is just a sport. You must keep remembering that. My marriage and my home are far more important.'

His wife, Rachel, is a model. It was to her that he dedicated the smiling gesture which followed his many famous victories, the tracing of the initial letters of 'I Love You' in the air. There was some tension when he ultimately left his Sussex home, to marry. 'I just found,' he says, 'that I was living an unreal existence, being fed and looked after by my mum at the age of 24.' But she wasn't, after all, his coach.

STEVE CRAM

In an age of the athlete as prima donna, as materialist and money-maker, as cynosure of the gossip columns, Steve Cram may seem a little too good to be true. In his quiet modesty, his unspoiled demeanour, his preference for the simple comforts of the north-east, his marriage in 1984 to his childhood sweetheart, he recalls older, gentler values.

As for his running, that, too, seems a little too good to be true. His ability, without the obvious finishing kick of an Ovett or a Coe, to plan each race to perfection, to stay with and see off the fastest opponent, to finish swift and strong, make him a frightening competitor, for all his amiability.

Emerging majestically from the shadow of Coe and Ovett in 1982, winning in turn the European and the Commonwealth 1,500 metres titles, Cram was expected to withdraw gracefully into that shadow when the two re-emerged the following year. Not a bit of it.

Despite a disastrous beginning to the season, when he stepped in a pothole in Colorado and trod on a soft drink can in his native north-east England, Cram won the world 1,500 metres title in Helsinki with a triumphant surge, added to it a further victory in the World Cup meeting at Crystal Palace, and went on to defeat Steve Ovett in a notable head-to-head contest, only just after Ovett had regained his 1,500 metres world record in Italy.

Still only in his early twenties, Cram must be favourite to win in Los Angeles the Olympic 1,500 metres title Coe took in Moscow. Blond, over six feet tall, slender and a powerful and elegant mover, he has given the lie to those who, even on the eve of the Helsinki success, were still saying that he lacked basic speed, and would do better in future to concentrate on the longer distances—perhaps even on the steeplechase, which Cram himself considers an event for failed middle-distance runners.

The son of a policeman and a German mother, Cram comes from a family that was chiefly interested in football. His uncle Bobby played for West Bromwich Albion, and it was hard at first to wean Cram from that game.

A little local coach, Jimmy Hedley of Jarrow, managed it, and the impressive example of another local man, the fine middle-distance runner Brendan Foster, did the rest. Between them, they have piloted Cram's remarkable career. Foster providing the international experience Hedley lacked, Cram meanwhile refusing to ditch his unfashionable coach for another one.

Cram was only 11 years old when Hedley spotted him, and his burgeoning promise, in a quarter-mile race. 'He wasn't particularly keen to run,' Hedley recalls. 'The whole family was steeped in football. I said, "Do you not fancy coming down for a little bit of training? It wouldn't do your football any harm." ' The day Hedley won his argument was perhaps the one when the young Cram competed in a race at South Shields. 'He didn't win. He got a pair of cuff links and I think he got the idea that every time he ran, he got a prize.'

Cram has stayed remarkably loyal to Hedley, although he says, much as Brendan Foster does, 'I wouldn't call him a coach any more, who wrote down on a piece of paper what I have to go and do. I think what happens is you often find when people become successful internationally, they start changing coaches. The person who brought them up isn't good enough any more; whereas I decided if Jimmy had got me that far, he obviously knew me best. Just because he couldn't tell me about the Olympic final didn't mean I couldn't do these things for myself.'

At the 1980 Moscow Olympics, Cram was very much the low man on the totem pole, behind Ovett and Coe. 'When I got in the race, I can't remember anything about it. I was down there thinking, Olympic final, isn't this great, and the gun went. I just wasn't switched on. I think I ran it in a daze.'

He had emerged triumphantly from that daze by 1982, when he scored his two famous victories, in the European Games and the Commonwealth Games. In the European Games, in Athens, one of his potential rivals, the strong young Scottish miler, Graham Williamson, crashed into a Spaniard in the 1,500 metres, fell, and was out of the race. 'I don't think it was particularly bad,' Cram says. 'It was just that one incident, in which Graham fell. I think I got so keyed up, the first two laps were like winding up an elastic band, and Graham falling was like letting it go. I'd decided that even if Graham should go to the front after 800 metres, I'd go to the front with 400 to go. When Graham fell, I was getting so wound up, it was like shooting a bullet out of a gun . . . I looked up at the scoreboard to see what had happened (*it was showing live images of the race*) and saw that I probably had a ten yard gap at that stage.'

In Brisbane, for the Commonwealth Games, Cram had treatment for a strained hamstring. In these circumstances, he was amazed that a field which included such experienced milers as John Walker of New Zealand and the Kenyan, Mike Boit, plus a number of young bloods with nothing whatever to lose, should not try to press him by setting the pace.

'Someone had clicked my heels for about the fifth time in the lap, and I was so angry I told them to go forth and multiply. From my point of view as an athlete, if I'd been a spectator, I think I'd have been disappointed in that race. It was just a jog for three laps, everybody just hanging around and waiting; they just accepted you were going to win, and wanted to be second or third. I can't understand why nobody made any move or tried anything different.'

SEBASTIAN COE

Glorious winner of the 1,500 metres final at the Moscow Olympics, after a disappointing failure in the 800 metres, Sebastian Coe is one more example of the athlete made articulate. He is not an Oxford man like Roger Bannister, having gone to Loughborough to continue his studies. But his approach to athletics is intelligent, fluent, humorous and detached.

Coe is also one of those slight, slender little men who, in the tradition of Wooderson rather than Bannister or Cram, make nonsense of the classical conception of the athlete. A rigorously exacting training programme over many years, tactical sense that only occasionally breaks down—as it did in the Moscow 800 metres—and a superb finishing burst have made him the great athlete that he is; even if the years 1982 and 1983 were, thanks first to injuries, then to a form of glandular illness, something of an anticlimax.

There has been a particular beauty in seeing Coe 'take off,' seeing, that is, so small a figure suddenly produce such dynamic power in the final straight, leaving other, bigger men hopelessly behind. 'I can never afford,' he said, 'to disregard the fact that my thing is running as fast as I possibly can for that last vital minute-and-a-half.'

Coe, who has flat feet, and thus doubly belies the image of the classical athlete, does what he described as 'only a moderate amount of distance work.' As against that, he spends hours every day in the gymnasium, stretching tendons, hamstrings, calves, loosening his lower back, squatting with enormous weights.

He has spoken of running the 5,000 metres in Los Angeles, and marvels at the fact that, despite dominating the 800 metres for years, he has never had a major title to show for it.

'I'll get arguments,' he has said, 'especially from milers and 1,500 metres runners, but I think 800 metres

is the hardest distance to get right. It's the last sprint, and not only do you have to call on both endurance and leg speed, but you've got to balance your two laps. In the mile, or 1,500 metres, you just have to make sure the third lap doesn't drop too much.' He believes, that 'If you get your preparation right for 800, then you will not be far off being okay for 1,500. If you make a mistake at 800, you're not likely to get a second chance. But at 1,500 metres, there are several routes to success; it's a more forgiving race, there's time to put errors right.'

How ironical, then, that major titles in the 800 metres have consistently eluded him. The 800 metres in Moscow, 1980, which he lost to Ovett, still represents, he admits, his 'biggest mistake'; tactically, he ran badly, and it was the eternal foe Ovett who took the gold, Coe of course having revenge in his beautifully judged 1,500 metres final.

Yet if this was his worst setback over the distance, there have been, surprisingly, so many others. There was the European Championship in Prague in 1978, and failure in the subsequent European Championship four years later in Athens. Then, however, there were extenuating circumstances. Coe had been suffering, aside from injuries, from glandular fever. In 1983, another frustrating year, the year of the first ever World Championships, it was a lymph gland that undermined him. He had toxoplasmosis.

With a characteristic philosophical attitude, however, he was not overly distressed by the failure in Athens. 'Athletics,' he says, 'is, of necessity, a very humbling sport. You are lucky to take out a fraction of what you put in. If anything, Athens was a good thing for me. Every sportsman needs to be brought up sharp, now and again. I'd had three marvellous years since 1979, with some luck in avoiding serious injury, and managing to get away with those injuries I did have. It would have been bad, on reflection, for me and for the sport to have come back from Athens with the 800 metres gold medal after only four weeks' makeshift preparation, having just missed eight weeks through injury. It would have devalued the significance of everything one is doing at a time of normal preparation. Because of Athens, because of the frustrations of last year, when I had two stress fractures at different times and then minor glandular illness, I think I am now even tougher mentally.'

But not proof, alas, against the glandular problems which sabotaged him, after one of those fatuous brushes with the athletics authorities which have so often disfigured the story of the sport in Britain. Initially, the 1,500 metres team for the Helsinki World Championships was announced without Coe; an enormous gaffe even if, in the event, his physical condition made his participation doubtful.

Much has been said about his relationship with Peter, his father and constant coach. There was perhaps a symbolic aspect to the moment, after his very disappointing run in an 800 metres race in Gateshead, shortly before the Helsinki meeting, when at the press conference Coe senior held a pair of running spikes in front of his son's face, apparently to silence him. Seb looked distressed and embarrassed, but he did not protest.

The relationship between great athlete and coach is difficult enough without its being complicated by the paternal bond. For those who have criticised Peter's dedicated, even compulsive, coaching, one can say only that it has brought the highest possible achievement. All the meticulous plans, the standing about on wet Sheffield winter nights with stopwatch in hand, produced not only one of the greatest athletes of all time, but did not prevent the emergence of a lively, intelligent, engaging young man.

ALBERT HILL — 800 and 1,500 metres gold, 1920

You might almost call Albert Hill the father of English mile and half-mile running. At the 1920 Antwerp Olympic Games he not only brought off the phenomenal double of 800 and 1,500 metres, but later became coach to a still finer miler, Sydney Wooderson.

Born in 1889, Hill was 31 when he ran in the Antwerp Olympics, and he had to compete in no fewer than seven races in eight days. It was 10 years since he had won his first British Championship—the four miles. Serving in World War I he survived to run even more successfully, taking the 880 yards and the mile titles in the first post-war AAA Championships of 1919. He also won the medley relay with his club, the Polytechnic Harriers.

The following year, not fully fit, he lost his AAA 880 yards title to the South African, Bevil Rudd, but in Antwerp he was back to his best, taking three medals. The silver came in the now defunct 3,000 metres team race.

He won the 800 metres final by a metre from the American, Earl Eby, in 1 minute 53.4 seconds (a British record), and beat another American, Ray, among others, in the 1,500 metres final.

The following year, he set a new British record for the mile of 4 minutes 13.8 seconds, which was a mere 1.2 seconds outside the world mark at that time. That was his swan song, and it came in the AAA Championships at Stamford Bridge. Afterwards he turned professional.

Showing no evident strain, Albert Hill races to a comfortable victory in the 1,500 metres final in the 1920 Olympics.

DOUGLAS LOWE — 800 metres gold, 1924, 1928

It was Douglas Lowe's stupendous achievement to win two successive Olympic gold medals for the 800 metres: in 1924, in Paris (when Abrahams and Liddell also won), and in 1928, in Amsterdam.

Born in 1902, 22 years old at the time of the Paris Olympiad, Lowe was not the favourite for the 800 metres. That distinction belonged to another Englishman, Henry Stallard. He had beaten Lowe less than a month before the Olympics in the AAA British national championships. In Paris, however, he had an injured foot, and although he did reach the final, he fell back in the finishing straight to fourth place.

This left Douglas Lowe to contest the victory with the Swiss, Paul Martin, and he duly won by 0.2 seconds in the record time for a British runner of 1 minute 52.4 seconds.

Two years after that, 25,000 spectators at London's Stamford Bridge saw him lose a memorable race to Germany's Dr Otto Peltzer, who set a new world record time of 1 minute 51.6 seconds. In the 1927 and 1928 AAA Championships Lowe achieved the double of the 440 and the 880, although suprisingly he was picked only for the 880 in the Amsterdam Olympics. Showing his flair for the great occasion, he duly won this event again. Lloyd Hahn of the United States, and the Frenchman Sera Martin, holder of the

Although favourite on neither occasion, Douglas Lowe won golds in 1924 and 1928.

world record of 1 minute 50.6 seconds, his two chief opponents, were the fastest men over the distance at that time. But Lowe rose to the occasion. Making his burst down the back straight, Lowe was ahead round the final bend and boldly kept his lead down the finishing straight to retain his title in a time of 1 minute 51.6 seconds. It was not a world record, but it set a new Olympic mark.

After that, Lowe retired—what else was left for him to attain? And for seven years he served as secretary of the AAA.

SYDNEY WOODERSON

Mile, 1930s and 1940s

In the triumphs of Wooderson one saw, in some sense, the victory of mind over matter, the will over the body, the tiny giant killer over the looming, lumbering giants. There seemed, before the race began, no possiblity that this little, scrawny man, so incongruous in shorts, spectacles and running vest, could challenge these Titans of the track. Dignity and impudence. Gods and a goblin. But how the goblin could run, above all when it came to the last, telling, killing quarter!

Had it not been for the war, Sydney Wooderson would probably have taken an Olympic gold medal. He was far and away the best British miler of his epoch and, even after the war was over, remained a middle distance runner capable of thrashing the finest Continental opposition.

Modest, diffident, deeply amateur—when he once found £12 in his bag after a meeting in Birmingham, he instantly sent it back—Wooderson had the superb finishing kick which distinguished the great miler, or for that matter the 800 metres or middle distance man.

He might have taken a gold for the 1,500 metres in the Berlin Olympics, but hurt an ankle so badly in the heats that he never reached the final, and eventually had to have an operation. Then 22, long years of excellence lay ahead of him.

The following year, he beat the world mile record with 4 minutes 6.4 seconds in a handicap race at Motspur Park. In 1938 he took the world record over 800 metres and 880 yards, the latter standing for 15 years.

Just after the war, in 1945, he ran his best mile ever at 4 minutes 4.2 seconds. The following year in Oslo came his magnificent victory in the 5,000 metres European Championship.

Sydney Wooderson's power shows clearly as he runs to break the half-mile record in 1938.

ROGER BANNISTER Mile, 1952 to 1954

Of Roger Bannister's running, his distinguished career, two images stay in the mind above all. First, the sight of him, triumphant, smiling and exhausted, immediately after breaking the tape at Iffley Road, to beat at last the 'impossible' four minute barrier for the mile, the scholar-athlete *in excelsis*. Second, later that same year of 1954, the moment in Vancouver, in the Final of the Commonwealth Games, when John Landy, his great Australian rival, looked left over his shoulder for Bannister, while Bannister went streaking past him on the right.

Though he made athletic history by breaking the four minute mile in May 1954 at Oxford, Roger Bannister competed in only one Olympic Games—Helsinki, 1952—and finished only fourth. Had there been an Olympics in 1954, however, he would surely have won the 1,500 metres.

Born in 1929 in Harrow, the son of an auditor-accountant, Bannister attended University College School, Hampstead, went up to Oxford as a 17-year-old, and won a slow mile in the Varsity match of 1947. 'There was no doubt about his innate ability,' recalled

Roger Bannister returns to the cheers of his fellow students after breaking the four-minute-mile in 1954.

Bannister's elegant style took him to the final in the 1952 Olympics.

Harold Abrahams. 'Here was the raw material from which champions are made.'

Just before the vital race at Iffley Road, where his Oxford contemporaries Chris Chataway and Chris Brasher were to pace him, it was to Abrahams that Bannister remarked, 'If the wind holds off, I believe I can do it.'

A runner who liked to train alone, and whose superb athletics career did not interfere with an equally distinguished one as a prize-winning medical student, Bannister liked to do without a coach. Yet the strange thing was that, on the way up to Oxford, he should derive great reassurance from finding Franz Stampfl, the celebrated Austrian coach who did so much for Brasher, in his railway compartment. Bannister couldn't 'bring himself to ask' advice, but he was 'delighted to see him'.

Iffley Road was no ideal place to attempt a record. The track of 'good cinders' was a slow one, and the wind was strong. It was Stampfl who told Bannister to run, that he could do it, that the wind might drop. Chataway, too, was encouraging. The wind dropped slightly: Bannister ran.

Brasher, after worrying Bannister by making a false start, set the pace perfectly in the first lap. After one and a half laps, Bannister heard Stampfl's voice shouting, 'Relax!' On the third lap, Chataway took the lead; at the start of the fourth, the time was 3:00.7. Then Bannister swept past Chataway and broke the tape in 3 minutes, 59.4 seconds.

'There was no pain,' he'd recall, 'only a great unity of movement and aim.'

He had not taken part in the 1948 Olympics, a decision for which he was criticised. The lack of experience, some fellow athletes felt, sabotaged him in the Helsinki games in 1952. On the day of the final, 'I hardly had the strength to warm up'. He kept the inside lane, 'too tired to struggle', got into second place, but, when he needed to make his burst, 'my legs were aching and I had no strength to force them faster'. It was Josey Barthel who won, Bannister ending in fourth place.

GORDON PIRIE
5,000 metres silver, 1956

The twilight of Gordon Pirie's career was to be seen in the twilight of the Olympic Stadium in Rome. As the sun set, so the long, lean figure dropped behind the field, giving up all faint hope of success. It had all been implicit on the nearby training track where his dogged interval training took place under his meticulous German coach.

Gordon Pirie was destroyed in the 1956 Olympics by the devastating running of Russia's Vladimir Kucs, and had lost his appetite for racing by the time it came to the Rome Olympiad, where he looked a forlorn figure. But in his time he was one of the finest runners in the world.

Born in Yorkshire in 1931, the son of a Scottish international athlete, he was inspired by Emil Zatopek's running in the 1948 Olympics. Pirie himself had carried the flame on one stage of the Olympics. Running up to 20 miles a day, sometimes in Army boots, he competed in the Helsinki Olympics, finishing fourth in the 5,000 metres and seventh in the 10,000 metres. There, he met the intense German coach, Waldemar Gerschler, whose repetition training he then embraced.

When he beat Zatopek over 5,000 and 10,000 metres in 1955, Pirie seemed to be favourite for one or even two gold medals in the 1956 Olympics. That June, he beat Kucs over 5,000 metres and set a new world record of 13 minutes 36.8 seconds.

Perhaps, as he admitted later, he shouldn't have challenged Kucs over the 10,000 metres, at which the Russian excelled, with a time that was 46 seconds better than Pirie's. Varying his pace ferociously, Kucs killed Pirie off— he finished in eighth place. Pirie went on to run a cautious race in the 5,000 metres (which Kucs won again) and he was clearly content with his silver medal.

In Rome in 1960, Pirie was eliminated in the heats of the 5,000 metres. He ran without joy, but clocked his best time ever in the 10,000 metres.

At his best, Gordon Pirie was one of the finest runners in the world.

DEREK JOHNSON   800 metres silver, 1956

Derek Johnson was an Oxford athletics blue from East London. He was also a medical student who became an expert in computers and a doughty and combative secretary of the International Athletes' Club. He will long be remembered for the glorious bid he made in the final of the 800 metres in the Melbourne Olympiad of 1956. He took the silver medal, but it was so nearly a gold. Later, lung trouble laid him low, but he was quite the finest British 800 metres runner there had ever been up to that time, and his commitment to the sport did not cease with his sadly premature retirement.

Harold Abrahams, himself a gold medal Olympic winner, generously said of Johnson after his splendid run in Melbourne: 'I have always regarded (him) as one of the greatest middle distance runners we have ever had in England.'

Abrahams gave an excellent description of the last stages of a thrilling final. Johnson's rivals were Boysen, a Norwegian, and two Americans, Courtney and Spurrier. Courtney came out best but it was a close thing.

With 100 metres left, Johnson was all but boxed in by Boysen and the two Americans. Running, as Abrahams put it, 'with perfect judgement and brilliant initiative,' Johnson suddenly saw a gap between the two Americans, and flashed through it. With but 50 metres to run, Johnson was about a foot ahead of Courtney, but the tall American, towering over him, 'called forth from his great reserve,' in Abrahams' words, 'and beat him by a stride.'

In Abrahams' view, it was a classic case of (in boxing terminology) a good big 'un beating a good little 'un. This theory may have been substantiated by the later victories of Peter Snell, but was severely questioned by the dominance of Coe over the same distance.

Ironically, Abrahams was one of those amateur athletics officials who later were to find Johnson a thorn in the flesh. Once, after being left out of a 400 metres relay team, he wrote to them saying that he would never run in another international until 'you stop treating athletes as half-witted performing monkeys, grateful for every peanut thrown their way.'

'The letter,' announced the Board, pompously secure in the knowledge that their selected team had won the title, 'has been returned to him, since it is couched in language that is abusive and intemperate, which renders the communication unacceptable.

In 1963, after recovering from tuberculosis, Johnson made a return to the track. He had no coach, and indeed had been coaching runners himself, but 'what I need is someone like Franz Stampfl (*Chris Brasher's Austrian coach*) with his thick accent, "Don't be stupid, you just go out and run!"'.

'I don't need a coach . . . I think as far as training and technique are concerned, there aren't many middle and long distance runners who *need* coaches, because these ideas, they're disseminated pretty rapidly throughout the athletics world. I think where one does need help really—coach isn't a good word for this—is occasionally at critical moments, where one suffers inevitable loss of confidence, where a man like Stampfl or Cerruty or Lydiard can make all the difference, and these moments can come in training and they can come immediately before very important races.'

There was no more important race in Johnson's short, distinguished career than the 800 metres final. Later he told Courtney that he had run and run that race over and over again, in his imagination, and had won it every time! Courtney replied that he had done the same.

Courtney, with his 6ft 2in frame, beat the Olympic record by 1.5 seconds. Johnson was just a tenth of a second slower.

Derek Johnson was regarded by many as one of the greatest British middle-distance runners of all time.

ANN PACKER 800 metres gold, 1964

Ann Packer's dazzling achievement in the Tokyo Olympics, where she won a gold in the 800 metres and a silver in the 400 metres, overshadowed the performance of her future husband, the British team captain, Robbie Brightwell. Eclipsed in the individual 400 metres, he gained some consolation with a glorious anchor lap for Britain in the 4 × 400 metres relay. He and Ann Packer had trained assiduously together, and he must take some credit for her triumphs in Tokyo, where her modest ambition had been merely 'to do well.'

There was a moment of pathos after Ann had taken second place in the 400 metres to Australia's Betty Cuthbert. Brightwell came to put a consoling hand on her shoulder, but she barely responded. That seemed to be that, because the 400 metres was her chief event. She had run her first 800 metres only six months before. After beating Betty Cuthbert in the semi-final of the 400 metres, she really seemed to have the gold medal within her grasp, but her time of 52.2 seconds (a British record) was two-tenths of a second slower than Cuthbert's time.

Ann Packer did get through her heat of the 800 metres the following day, but with difficulty. There was still no hint of what was about to happen. But in the semi-final Ann, now running with much more confidence and perhaps helped by the lack of pressure, knocked 6.2 seconds off her previous time.

In the final itself, with 200 metres to go, Ann was apparently out of the reckoning. Then, with stupendous acceleration, she went past the field, to win in a world record time of 2 minutes 1.1 seconds. It was one of the most surprising victories of the Olympiad in which Britain, captained splendidly by Brightwell, did so well.

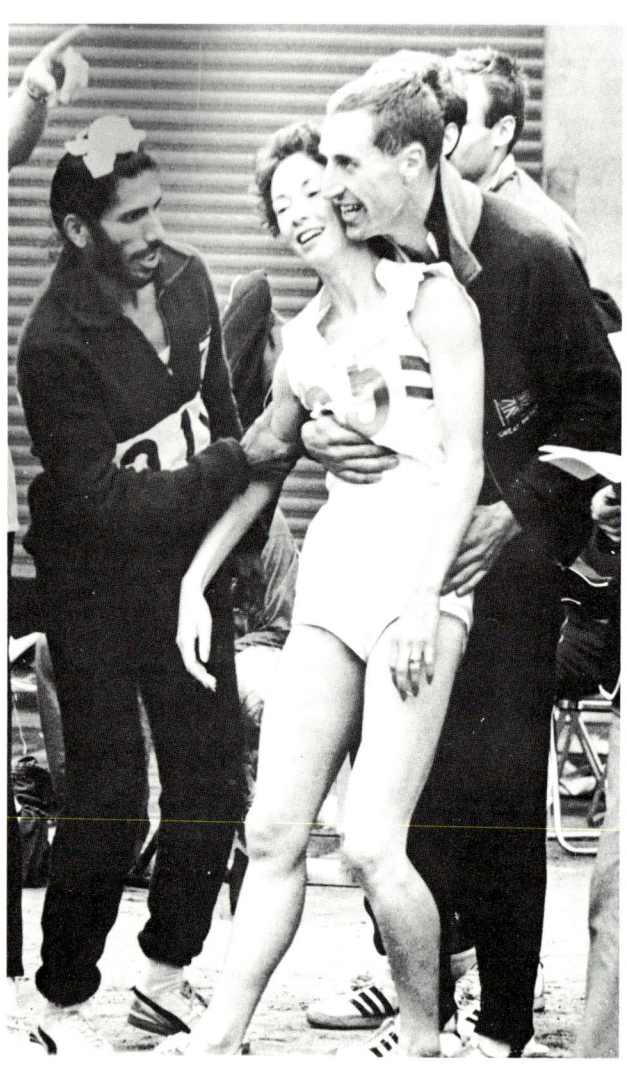

Ann Packer relaxes against her team captain and fiancé, Robbie Brightwell, after winning the 800 metres gold.

ALLAN WELLS

When Allan Wells dipped forward at the tape to win the 100 metres final of the Olympic Games in Moscow in 1980, he was unconsciously repeating the very movement of Harold Abrahams, the last Briton to win the title, 56 years earlier, in Paris. In the stands, meanwhile, Wells's devoted wife Margot, herself a coach and international athlete, was crying, 'Come on, Allan! Come on, Allan!' like a soul in pain.

It was an astonishing achievement for the deep chested, heavily muscled, 28-year-old Scot, a relatively late starter in the turbulent field of international athletics. He is a man who has allied to his great physical strength a dedication remarkable even among the athletes of the present, committed, generation. Certainly money was never the aim, the true goal. As Wells once wryly pointed out himself, a moderate Scottish professional footballer would have earned, for most of his career, substantially more.

Wells, an Edinburgh man, began as a long jumper, and for a while ran the 400 metres before at last concentrating on the sprints. There have been various coaches in his career (he tends to leave them, for he is not the most tranquil of people), but perhaps the one who gave him the most apart from Margot ('He's the running brain, I'm his eyes') was the former Powderhall professional sprinter, Wilson Young.

Wells embraced the unorthodox training method of working out on a speed ball, like a boxer; and how he worked out! He has been known to throw as many as 4,600 punches in one training stint. He was unorthodox, too, in the way that for years he eschewed the use of starting blocks; but there was nothing left to chance in the way he ran his major races.

In Moscow, where he saw off Cuba's formidable Silvio Leonard in the 100 metres, Wells had anything but an easy draw, running in lane eight, with the wind especially hard to contend with. 'I ran a thinking race,'

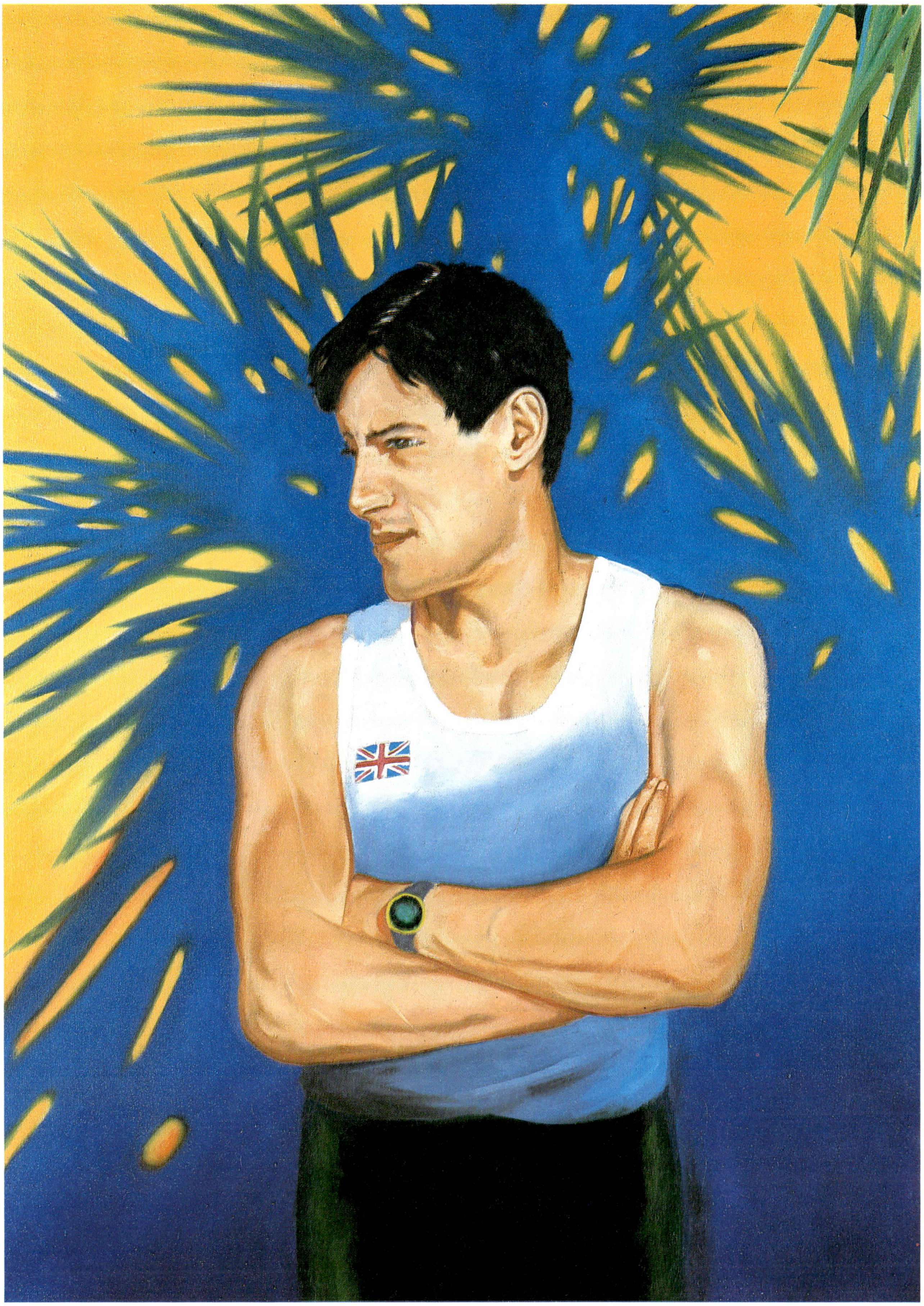

he says. But perhaps he was more impetuous in the subsequent 200 metres when Italy's Pietro Paolo Mennea, one of those he had beaten, had his revenge by edging Wells into second place.

And how often Wells has done just that! His determination and courage are such that he can never be written off; even after a disappointing season such as 1982, when so many things went against him. But he had the strength of mind to skip the European Games, get himself back into his finest form, then superbly win the 100 metres in Brisbane, and go on to dead-heat with a fellow Briton in the 200 metres.

Having turned to the two sprints as late as 1976, Wells had left his Powderhall sprint champion, and coach, Wilson Young, by the time he excelled in the Edmonton Commonwealth Games. There he won two gold medals, one for the individual 100 metres, and the other for the relay together with the Scottish team. He also won the silver in the individual 200 metres.

Unlike his great rival Mennea, who has stayed with the same coach, Vittori, almost since boyhood, and has always treated him with immense deference, Wells tends to need change and breaks off such relationships somewhat abruptly.

'Sprinting is all about aggression and confidence', he says. 'If for one second you think you are going to get beaten, then you might as well forget it. Certain people in the past have really annoyed me, and I have taken pent-up aggression on to the track. Scots are sometimes classed as naturally aggressive. I don't know if it's true, but certainly aggression helps me. I get a certain exhilaration from running fast, but it is a cut-throat business. There's a lot of pressure. You've got to do it there and then. One mistake in Moscow and I've had it,' he forecast, perhaps superfluously as it transpired, at least insofar as the 100 metres was concerned. 'There's no second chance.'

After that victory, he observed 'The training has to be right and serious, and mine has been, but all the strength of your body isn't enough if you don't have a good head on your shoulders. . . . I was drawn in lane eight, where the wind was most awkward, and just about everything was against me, but I stayed cool and did a job.'

In fact, running great races against the wind was something he had been doing for a long time; not least before the Edmonton Games, when the obligation to run into the wind had affected his times and thus, perhaps providentially, camouflaged from the athletics world at large just how well he had been running. Thus his dynamic form in the Commonwealth tournament came as a great surprise to some of his rivals.

After his Moscow victory, Margot paid tribute to her husband's vast dedication. 'I've watched this man drinking his own sweat,' she said, 'working his heart out in the rain and the snow, everything.'

Carl Lewis and the brilliant Americans forced him out of the medals in the Helsinki world championships of 1983, where Mennea beat him, too. But he had his revenge on Mennea soon afterwards at the Crystal Palace. And in Los Angeles, even at this late stage of Wells' career, perhaps he can surprise the world again.

But whether he wins or not, the surviving, vibrant memory of Wells will be that of throbbing power, calculation obscured by sheer locomotion. Locomotive, indeed, is a word that comes easily to mind. The thundering muscularity of his progress would seem, on his best days, irresistible. He may have dipped at the tape like Abrahams, but there resemblance ends. In Wells, effort, sheer force, was made manifest. He was and is a superb machine, made inexorably to run.

HAROLD ABRAHAMS

100 metres gold, 1924

It was perhaps inevitable and appropriate that Harold Abrahams, gold medallist turned journalist and administrator, should show such sympathy towards Roger Bannister, 30 years after his own success. Both were Oxbridge men and each was looked at a mite askance for being so 'serious' about his sport. But where Abrahams had his own personal coach, Bannister tried to do without one.

The film *Chariots of Fire* has revived interest in the prowess of Harold Abrahams and his glorious success in the Olympic 100 metres final in Paris in 1924. Yet it said nothing of his achievements in the long jump, in which he set a record that endured for 33 years. His 1924 leap cleared 24 feet 2½ inches. Sadly, his fine career virtually came to an end the year after his Olympic triumph. He broke a leg jumping at Stamford Bridge, the Chelsea football ground.

Educated at Repton and Caius College Cambridge, Abrahams came from a remarkably gifted Anglo-Jewish family. One brother was medical officer to the British athletics team, and another was an Olympic long jumper like Harold himself. But neither had his sublime flair as a sprinter.

When he went up to Cambridge, he already possessed a reputation as a public school athlete. He at once established himself as a university star,

Harold Abrahams broke the tape to win the 100 metres gold in the 1924 Paris Olympics with his characteristic and controversial swoop.

while spending much time helping a group of young working men to produce plays, magazines, and sports meetings. The rather dour figure of later years, excoriated by current athletes as the Grey Eminence of the long-suffering chief athletics administrator Jack Crump, lay far in the future.

A true amateur in essence, Abrahams nevertheless became a controversial figure by bringing what some of his contemporaries disapprovingly regarded as a 'professional' approach to his sport. He proceeded to hire a personal coach named Sam Mussabini, and trained with a dedication unknown to, and somewhat mistrusted by, the Corinthian bloods of his day. Mussabini told him, 'Only think of two things—the report of the pistol and the tape, and when you hear one, run like hell for the other.'

His first, valuable experience of an Olympiad came in 1920 in Antwerp, when he participated in no fewer than four events. By 1924 he was 24, but in the Paris Olympics, few gave him—or his rival, Eric Liddell, who refused to compete in the Sunday final on religious grounds—much chance against the fabulous Americans. After all, no European had ever won the 100 metres dash. After Abrahams' feat, no European would win it again until the Rome Olympic Games of 1960.

But in the second heat and in the semi-finals, Abrahams ran like a hare, equalling the Olympic record of 10.6 seconds set up, astonishingly enough, in the semi-final of the 1912 Stockholm Games by the American Donald Lippincott.

In later years Abrahams claimed, not surprisingly, that the semi-final represented his finest piece of sprinting. He came from behind in a manner phenomenal in so short a distance. The powerfully built American Charlie Paddock gained a two metre lead on him early in the race, but as a great sprinter and Olympic champion of the future, Mennea, would say, the man who starts best is not necessarily the man who leads at the end.

With 50 metres left, Abrahams was still a metre behind Paddock, but then, with a marvellous surge, he made up the distance and won. Each of the two athletes had a controversial finish. Abrahams had been criticised for his 'rhythm-breaking' drop finish, his hawklike swoop, as he thrust back his arms like the wings of a bird and dropped his chest against the tape. Paddock, in contrast, finished with a kind of long jump, a fractional pause followed by a leap for the line.

Paddock and Abrahams were scheduled to run in the final that Sunday afternoon, barely four hours after contesting the semi-final. Also in the race were New Zealander Arthur Porritt, (an Oxford blue and later a distinguished surgeon), and three more

Abrahams' speed allowed him to become the first European to beat the Americans who dominated the field in the 100 metres.

Americans: Loren Murchison, Chester Bowman and the formidable newcomer Jackson Scholz, who had won the other semi-final. To fill in the long, tense hours, Mussabini took Abrahams on a protracted drive through the streets of Paris. Few athletes, even the devoted Americans, could have been better prepared than Abrahams, who even knew the precise number of strides he took in any 100 metres race. His brilliant dash in the semi-final suggested he could knock two-tenths of a second off the record.

It was five past seven in the evening before the athletes at last lined up for the final, with Abrahams in lane four, after Paddock, Scholz and Murchison. This time Abrahams made a much better start, but there was still no clear leader until just before the halfway mark, when Abrahams drew powerfully away, to win by a metre with his familiar ground-gaining, controversial swoop. Porritt took the bronze.

Abrahams, called to the Bar, later joined the National Parks Commission and was for many years treasurer of the British Amateur Athletics Board, athletics correspondent of the *Sunday Times*, and a noted broadcaster.

ERIC LIDDELL — 400 metres gold, 1924

With Harold Abrahams, Eric Liddell was celebrated in the film, *Chariots of Fire*. He was a magnificent athlete, being a Scottish International rugby player as well as an Olympic runner. He was also a deeply religious man whose beliefs took him into missionary work in China, and led to his tragic death in a Japanese prison camp during World War II. It was 1945, and he was still only 43 years old.

Would Liddell have won the 100 metres in Paris, had it not been run on a Sunday? He was astonishingly versatile. In 1923 he set an English record for the 100 yards of 9.7 seconds which stood for another 35 years. To this British title he also added the 220 yards. But when he learned that the 100 metres race in Paris would be run on the Sabbath, he withdrew.

'He's a traitor to his country,' said reporters. Liddell retorted, 'It's just my belief. . . . I'm not going to run on the Lord's day; that's that.'

So Liddell, contested the 400 metres instead—a distance over which he had never run faster than 49 seconds. The Olympic record stood at 48.2 seconds, and it was broken in the second heat by Joseph Imbach of Switzerland, who returned 48 seconds dead. But Liddell himself got better all the time. He clocked 48.2 seconds in the second semi-final, still slower than the winning time in the first semi-final in which the American Horatio Fitch returned 47.8 seconds. But in the final, Liddell surpassed himself. Drawn in the outside lane, he was away like a stag, covering the first 200 metres in a remarkable 22.2 seconds. Having built up such a lead, he held on to it down the home straight to break the tape four or five yards ahead, in 47.6 seconds. It was a world record for the 400 metres.

Liddell's pace was a triumph over his awkward style—his knee lift seemed too high and uneconomical and his arms whirled about in the air. But his drive was formidable. Fellow students described how he would run smoothly until the last stages of a 400 metres or 440 yards race. 'Then the head went back, the elbows went up; but when that happened, the rest of the race might as well say, we give up!'

DALEY THOMPSON

The greatest all round athlete of his generation, perhaps of all time, Daley Thompson is a blend of the exuberant and the suspicious, the extravert and the 'loner', a man overtly full of *joie de vivre* and confidence who can withdraw, suddenly, into a cagey solitude, refuse to carry ceremonial flags, snub importunate reporters, and seem happy and at ease only in the company of a few Gargantuan intimates.

Thompson announced in Nice before the 1980 Olympic Games that there was no doubt at all that he would win the Olympic gold medal for the decathlon in Boston. So he did, with a panache and a superiority which put the medal in his pocket before the last event, his much disliked 1,500 metres, allowing him to trot round happily in his own time. Since then he has added his second Commonwealth Games decathlon medal, in Brisbane, having previously and splendidly won in Edmonton, Canada, and thrown in the first ever world title in Helsinki in 1983 for good measure. Thompson must be favourite to take his second Olympic gold medal in Los Angeles. He will still be barely 26 years old. It is a measure of his love for the decathlon that he has refused to cash in on his Olympic success as his predecessor and mentor, the American, Bruce Jenner, did after his 1976 success in Montreal.

Winning the event in Edmonton, with a first day record, and an eventual second best world pointage, he insisted on all his competitors joining him in a lap of joy and honour. Four years later, he would be criticised for refusing to carry the flag in the opening ceremony; you could call it a diplomatic lapse, a measure of his single-mindedness. In any event, he won the title again.

In 1982, he also won the European title in Athens, defeating Jurgen Hinsen of West Germany, who only a month earlier had broken his world record. In 1983's world championships in Helsinki, Thompson said his

43

German opponents snubbed him in the athletes' village. It was the kind of spur he needed to win another famous victory. Thompson can pole vault over 16 feet, long jump over 26 feet, run 10.6 seconds for the 100 metres; but the event he most likes to watch is the high hurdles. He's the supreme competitor.

There are curious contradictions in Daley's approach to his sport and to his life at large. Thus, at a time when diet was becoming more and more important, more and more carefully studied and monitored, Daley at the height of his career was largely existing on junk food, hamburgers, four at a time, and drinking quantities of Coca Cola. On the other hand, Thompson, beneath an apparently flippant and casual exterior, is a man ultimately, almost professionally, dedicated to athletics, who has read almost everything, including Zen, about the conditioning of the competitor's mind.

It is interesting that the far less ebullient, though equally single-minded, Steve Ovett should plainly be his favourite athlete; he was terribly disappointed that Coe and not Ovett should have won the 1,500 metres gold medal in Moscow, while he himself became the first Briton ever to win the decathlon. Victory for Ovett, he thought, would have put the seal on him as the greatest middle-distance runner of his epoch.

'I refuse,' Thompson has said, 'even to contemplate defeat. I was talking to Steve Ovett one day about what drove us on, and I told him that really I was the kind of guy who felt he should have been born Sir Somebody Something, and now I was out to show that I deserved recognition through sheer ability. Steve just nodded and said, "Oh, yes, that's your working class syndrome showing through." On reflection, I suppose he has a point.'

Perhaps. But the working class syndrome, whatever that is, has never produced an athlete like Daley Thompson in the history of British sport. It is strange to think that he might well have become a professional footballer; when at Farney Close School, Bolney, that was his ambition. The West London clubs Chelsea and Fulham both gave him trials, but neither signed him on. So it was that, at the instigation of his headmaster, in his very last school term, he joined the local athletics club, and in no time at all was competing as a sprinter in the English Schools Championship. 'I went along there,' he confesses, 'thinking I was the bee's knees; up until then, I reckoned it was going to be a walkover. I came fourth. It put a big dent in my ego.'

So much so that another disillusionment, in the AAA Junior Championship, moved him to try soccer once again. It was at this point that Bob Mortimer, of the Essex Beagles Athletic Club, may have changed the course of decathlon history; for he persuaded Thompson to change his mind, and to give athletics another shot. The following year, Thompson triumphed in both the meetings which initially had so disappointed him. He won the 200 metres in the Schools Championship and the 100 metres in the AAA junior event. Then it was that Mortimer made another, quite crucial, suggestion; that Thompson, with his splendid physique and outstanding natural ability, should consider the decathlon.

Tom McNab, then the national coach, might well have talked him out of it again when he tried to dissuade Thompson from participating in his first course, because he thought he would never be a good enough sprinter to survive in the decathlon. By this time, however, Thompson had the wind in his sails, and sailed past such objections. 'Tom,' he said, shortly before he removed all doubts of his prowess by winning the Olympic title in Moscow, 'is naturally a lovable guy, and we were to become close friends. Needless to say, I've never let him forget that first opinion.'

JUDY LIVERMORE

This lithe, charming girl must, if she is to win any kind of heptathlon medal in Los Angeles, learn to build on her splendid starts. As things stand, the events in which she does best, such as the hurdles and the high jump—in which she is outstanding by any criterion—come on the first day. Then come the events in which she is less gifted, and anticlimax can ensue.

In the World Championships at Helsinki in 1983, she was leading the field after most of the first day. Then came an unhappy performance in the 200 metres, and things began to go wrong. She came down to fourth place overnight, and the following day was disastrous. She had no doubt been haunted by the bizarre experience of the javelin when she carelessly picked up the wrong one, not heeding the colour code. As a result, she found herself trying to throw a javelin intended for much longer-throwing competitors. So it was that the javelin kept landing butt end instead of on its point, thus giving Judy no points at all.

If she can reach her best form in the 200 metres, and improve her performance in the javelin, 800 metres and long jump, then she might surprise us all in Los Angeles.

A six-footer from Nuneaton, studying sociology, Judy's very warmth and ease of temperament may be against her in a dour world where East European female athletes gobble steroids and are not unknown to partake of testosterone. Those who criticise Judy's allegedly easy-going attitude might bear in mind that she is an athlete of the highest class who has remained a lively and engaging young woman.

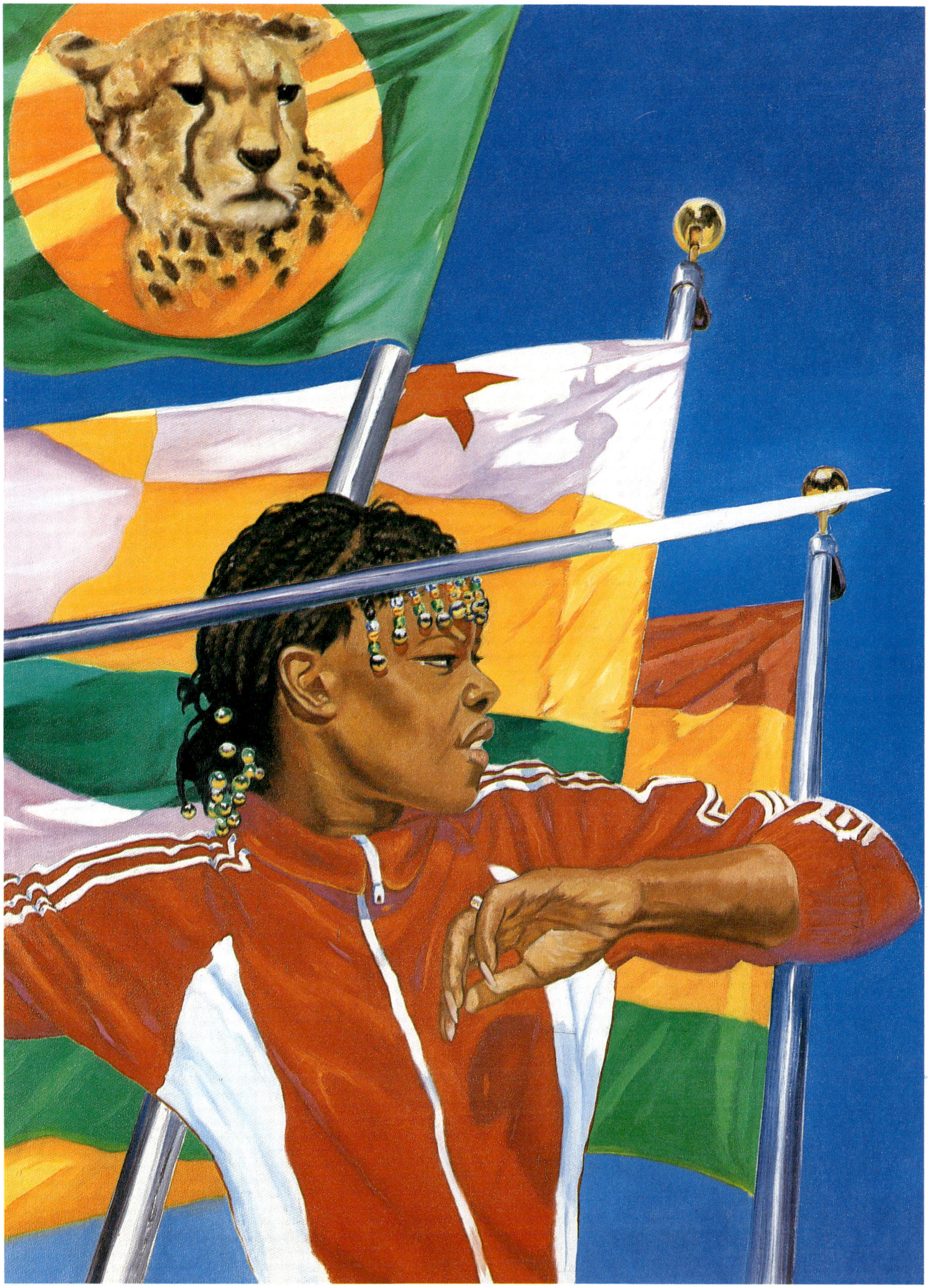

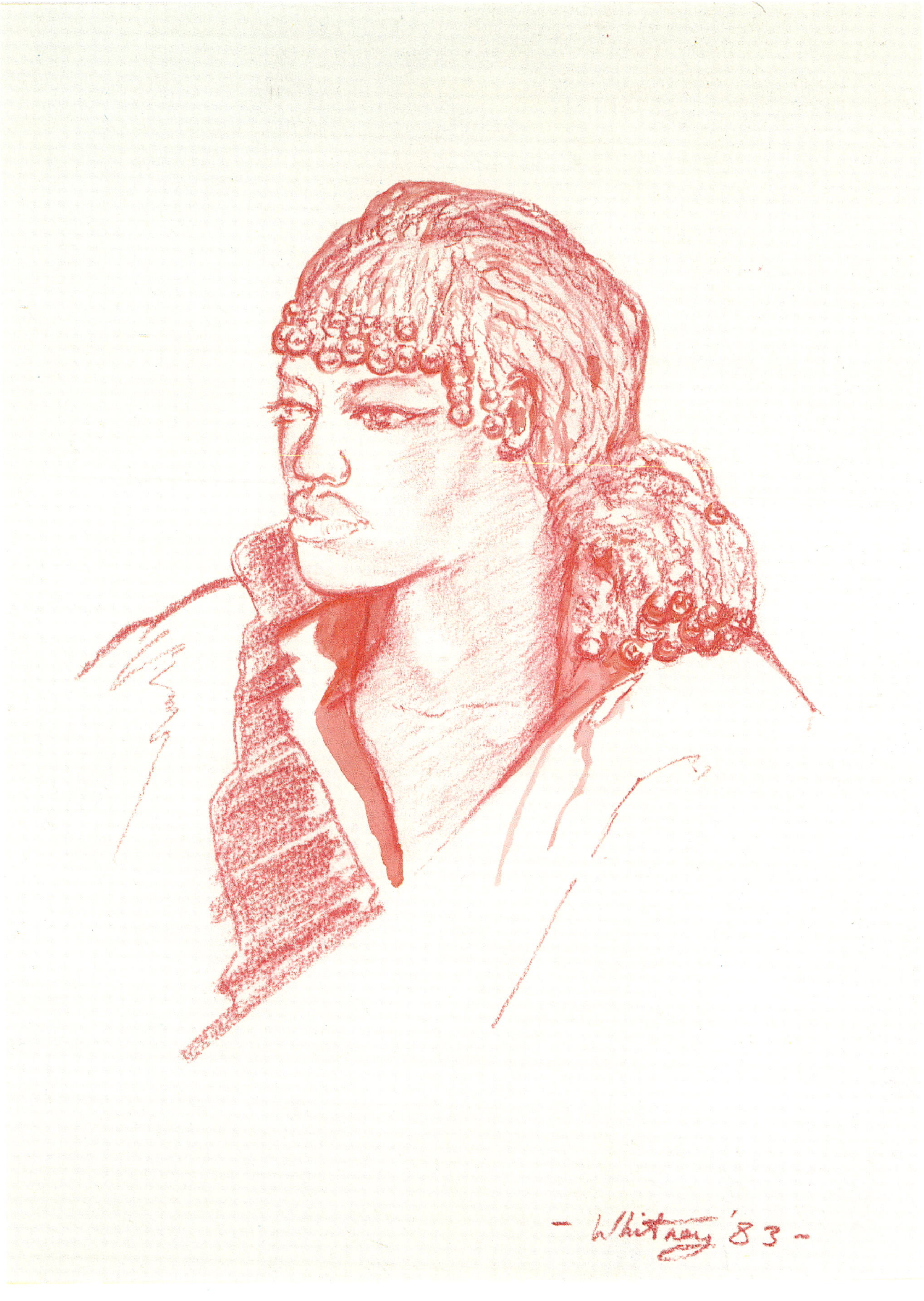
- Whitney '83 -

49

FATIMA WHITBREAD

Only 5 feet 5½ inches tall, although extremely robust in the upper body, Fatima Whitbread was chosen British woman athlete of the year in 1983 by the country's writers on athletics. It was in recognition of her extraordinary javelin throw in the World Championships in Helsinki, which so nearly won her a gold medal at the expense of the red-hot Finnish favourite, Tiina Lillak. It was only with her final throw that, to the thunderous relief of the home crowd, Miss Lillak accomplished the throw that beat the 69.14 metres Fatima had achieved with her very first throw.

The irony of it was that the 22-year-old Fatima, from Thurrock in Essex, had not even reached the qualifying distance of 62 metres on the previous day, and was allowed to take part in the final only because there was a dearth of competitors.

That 69.14 metres was not quite the best she had done, and certainly not the best that had been done by another fine English javelin thrower, Tessa Sanderson, whose unusual ability in the event has not been complemented by the perfect temperament. Nor, when things went wrong for her in the qualifying competition in the Moscow Olympics, did she have Fatima's subsequent luck in Helsinki.

It has been Fatima's fortune that Margaret Whitbread, whose adopted child she is, was not only a fine javelin thrower in her own day, but also a senior coach of both men and women, and has guided her career. Fatima, who is also an excellent hockey player, believes that women javelin throwers do not reach their best until they are 24. This seems to augur well for Los Angeles.

51

LORD BURGHLEY

Hurdles gold, 1928

How appropriate it was that when David Hemery so splendidly won the 400 metres hurdles Olympic gold medal for Britain in Mexico City in 1968, it should be presented to him by the Marquess of Exeter, Lord David Cecil Burghley, who had won the same medal in Amsterdam 40 years before.

Lord Burghley, who later became one of the leading administrators both in British athletics and in the Olympic movement, competed in three Olympic Games. He ran the 110 metres hurdles in Paris in 1924, where he was knocked out in a strong first round heat. In 1932 in Los Angeles, he participated not only in both hurdles races, taking an estimable fourth place in the 400 metres, but also in the 4 × 400 metres relay, in which he helped Great Britain to win the silver medal. His time in the 400 metres final of 52.2 seconds was a British record at that point.

His superb victory in Amsterdam, at the age of 23, broke what had until then been an American stranglehold on the event. He continued to compete at the highest level for another five years, when he lost his 440 yards British hurdles title to the talented Italian, Luigi Facelli.

In the British Empire Games of 1930, in Hamilton, Ontario, Lord Burghley won gold medals in both the hurdles events, and also in the 4 × 440 yards relay.

Lord Burghley raced to a superb victory in the 400 metres hurdles in Amsterdam in 1928.

Lord Burghley presented the medals at many international events.

CHRIS BRASHER

Steeplechase gold, 1956

When Chris Brasher, coached by Franz Stampfl, won the 3,000 metres steeplechase gold medal in the Olympic Games at Melbourne in 1956—after a long and nerve-wracking hiatus before his win was confirmed—it was the stuff of fairy tale. Here was the Oxford runner who had always played second fiddle, the devoted pacemaker, to his more talented contemporaries, Roger Bannister and Chris Chataway, doing what neither of them was ever able to do: win an Olympic final. It was said by a fellow Olympic runner who sat beside them that the two of them watched the finish of the race in stony-faced silence.

Brasher's willpower is implicit in the very sound of his voice, strange and strained, suggesting eventual victory over what, in anybody else, might well have been a stammer. It was this willpower that made him such a superb competitor and enabled him to win an Olympic gold when his far more talented contemporaries failed. Perhaps, too, it was implicit in the manner of the race he ran, the unbridled effort and challenge that enabled him to battle his way home and caused groundless objections to be raised.

Yet he himself would be the first to pay tribute to his mentor, the Austrian coach Franz Stampfl, so much heeded and admired by the Oxbridge athletes of his day.

Astonishingly, Brasher had never

won a national championship or any major national event. Born in Georgetown, Guyana in 1928, and educated at Radley public school, he had been overshadowed even in British steeplechase running by John Disley and Eric Shirley, each of whom, when it came to the 1956 Olympic final, had better times behind them than he.

But four years earlier, running for Britain in the Helsinki Olympics in his first international, he had shown his grit and his response to the great occasion. Disley took the bronze medal, but Brasher, although hurt in the second lap, had the courage to complete the race. He has been wont to quote the great athlete who said that you can never win anything major unless there have been moments in your career when you thought you were going to die.

When Roger Bannister broke the four-minute-mile barrier at Oxford in 1954, it was Brasher who cleverly and selflessly paced him for the first two-and-a-half laps, shrewder at the time than even Bannister realised. In 1956, he showed his potential by coming second to Disley in the steeplechase in a match against the Czechs, returning his best time of 8 minutes 47.2 seconds.

His time in Melbourne was 8 minutes 41.2 seconds, good enough to beat the four men in the race who'd run faster in the past than he. He calculated his race cleverly, winning with a powerful surge, 300 metres from home.

But 30 minutes after his success, there was the shattering announcement that he had been disqualified for obstruction. There were more than two hours to wait before the unfortunate Brasher heard that an appeal jury had overruled the decision, deciding that the obstruction had been inadvertent, and that his victory stood.

Within no time at all, he became Sports Editor of the *Observer* Sunday newspaper, and passed from there successfully into television. Mountaineering and orienteering are other sports in which he later engaged.

MARY (BIGNAL) RAND — Long jump gold, 1964

This lithe and pretty girl failed almost inexplicably in the long jump event at the Rome Olympics of 1960, but won the event triumphantly in Tokyo four years later, when she had become better used to the harsh pressures of an Olympiad. She also distinguished herself in the pentathlon.

A plumber's daughter from Wells, in Somerset, where the length of her winning long jump is picked out in gold letters on the pavement, Mary Bignal, as she originally was, benefited from the system of athletic scholarships at Millfield School, in her native county.

She was a splendid all-round athlete, who took part in 63 international events for Great Britain, including both sprints, the long jump, the high jump, and the 80 and 100 metres hurdles. At 16 she won two women's AAA intermediate titles, and at 17 won the high jump in an international match against Poland, jumping 5 feet 5 inches. The following year, she competed for Britain in the pentathlon in the Stockholm European Championships, finishing seventh but setting a British record of 4,466 points.

So to Rome, where she graced the Olympic village, charmed everybody, and led the long jump qualifiers with 20 feet 9¼ inches. But she froze in the final, among the intimidating competitors with their two-way radios illicitly tuned to their coaches. She had two no-jumps, jumped no better than 19

feet 8½ inches in the end, and finished a demoralized ninth. But she did recover sufficiently to take fourth place, one tenth of a second short of a bronze, in the 80 metres hurdles final.

Married by then to the oarsman Sydney Rand, Mary won bronze European Championship medals in 1962 in the long jump and 400 metres relay.

In Tokyo, she was again a favourite for the long jump, and the other girls in the team, especially Pat Pryce and Mary Peters, did all they could the night before the event to keep her cheerful and relaxed, laughing about the way they would soon be dazzled by the gold medal hanging from the wall.

Once again she began splendidly in the qualifying rounds, this time setting a new Olympic record of 21 feet 7¼ inches. Her first jump in the final showed that there would be no problem this time with her temperament, for she bettered her own record by another quarter of an inch. Her fourth jump set yet a third record, an inch-and-a-half better, and in the fifth round, her phenomenal 22 feet 2¼ inches won the gold: the first time any woman had jumped over 22 feet. She was 6 inches ahead of her closest competitor, Poland's versatile Irena Kirszenstein.

To this gold, she added a silver medal in the pentathlon, in which she beat the world record, and finished 211 points behind the winner. A bronze medal followed, in the 4 × 100 metres relay. In 1965, she was awarded the MBE in the New Year's Honours List.

Injury prevented her competing in the 1968 Olympics. The following year, she married the American decathlon champion, Bill Toomey, and settled in California, triumphant proof that a delightfully feminine girl could compete on level terms with the hulking Amazons of modern athletics.

If there is a moral, and a message, for women competitors to be drawn from the colossally successful career of Mary Rand, it is surely that you can succeed, even at the highest level, the most furiously competitive peak, of athletics, without resigning grace and femininity. There was, even in Mary's failure in Rome, a kind of enchanting pathos, a feeling she had come to grief because she was a girl, and a pretty one, not an automaton. Then, in Tokyo, she excelled. She had had her cake and eaten it to the last crumb.

LYNN DAVIES — Long jump gold, 1964

Lynn Davies's gold medal in the long jump in the Tokyo Olympics of 1964 was a tribute to his own confidence and determination. In appallingly wet weather conditions, the 22-year-old Welshman outjumped more highly regarded rivals, such as the reigning Olympic champion Ralph Boston. Boston was widely expected to win again: a month earlier, he had jumped a massive 27 feet 10½ inches, even though the jump had been wind assisted. By contrast, Davies himself had never jumped farther than 26 feet 4 inches.

It was only the previous year that Davies, under the coaching of Ron Pickering, had changed from what was known as the hang method of long jumping to the hitch kick—a two-and-a-half hitch kick while travelling through the air. He was very fast, which helped, and he got even faster, knocking four-tenths of a second off his 100 yards time, to clock 9.5 seconds. So it was that he managed to jump over 26 feet, and establish himself as an Olympic contender.

A trip to the United States Championships was hardly reassuring. Davies finished no higher than sixth, but he did not let that demoralize him; rather did he use the experience to his eventual advantage. It is odd to reflect that he might instead have been competing in the triple jump, an event for which he had shown great talent, jumping as much as 50 feet 7½ inches, before a series of injuries forced him to give it up and turn to the long jump.

Davies's strength served him well in the cold, wet, heavy conditions, complicated by a strong wind. Yet it wasn't until his last qualifying jump that he squeezed into the final; and it was with his fifth jump that he achieved a splendid 26 feet 5¾ inches, his best jump ever at the most important time, to take the title and beat Boston.

Before the contest, Ralph Boston had

said, 'I don't like being favourite, but if that's how it is, that's how it's got to be.'

'What did encourage me,' Davies said, after he had won, 'was Boston's persistent grumbling about the weather conditions. Because you regard a man like Boston as infallible, and as soon as you see a weak chink in his armour, you're glad.' When it came to his fifth, winning jump, Davies was lying third, 'and I thought, it's this jump, hell or bust. If it was a big jump, I knew I could get ahead . . . and as soon as I'd jumped it, I came back to the other competitors and Boston said, "That'll get you the gold." But hell and high water, I couldn't look at the pit, especially for a long time, when there was Boston's jump. There was a hush from the crowd, then it went up on the scoreboard; four centimetres less! But the worst moment of all was when I nearly failed to qualify in the morning. I was about ready to give up in the wind and the rain, and the ground was like a quagmire. And I thought, I've done all this bloody weight lifting, I won't let it go for nothing.'

There wasn't much he could do about Bob Beamon's fabulous 29 feet 2½ inch jump in the thin air of Mexico City, four years later. Davies himself finished only ninth with a leap of 26 feet and half an inch; but he did beat Beamon the following year, at a lower altitude, in Stuttgart.

DAVID HEMERY

Hurdles gold, 1968

Cometh the hour, cometh the man. David Hemery's staggering 48.1 seconds in the final of the 400 metres hurdles in Mexico City not only won him the gold medal, but beat the American Geoff Vanderstock's new record by 0.7 seconds. Needless to say, he also smashed the Olympic record set by Glenn Davis in Rome, eight years earlier.

Tall, blond and slender, Hemery was one of those English athletes who owed much of their success to the fact that they went to college, trained and competed in the United States. He did not make any great impact in his event until a couple of years before the 1968 Olympics, winning the Commonwealth Games 120 yards hurdles event in 14.1 seconds in Kingston, Jamaica, and getting to the semi-finals of the European Championships. At Boston

University, the skilled coaching of Bill Smith was as great a help as that of the once successful British pole vaulting champion, Fred Housden, who had closely and shrewdly studied the technique of hurdling.

Hemery beat two of his main American challengers, Vanderstock and Boyd Gittins, in a time of 49.8 seconds in the American collegiate championships, then went back to England and bettered that with a time of 49.6 seconds. Both his challengers and their compatriot Ron Whitney, however, had run faster than that.

When it came to Mexico City, Hemery judged his effort perfectly. The three hurdle races, up to and including the final, were staged on three successive days. Hemery did not over-exert himself on the first two days, being content to come second to the Italian, Roberto Frinolli, in his heat, and actually finishing no better than third out of four in his semi-final, though his 49.3 seconds time equalled the British record set in the other semi-final by John Sherwood.

Frinolli, Whitney and Vanderstock got to the final, together with a Russian deaf mute, a couple of West Germans, and the two Englishmen. Hemery got away beautifully, although it wasn't until the sixth of the ten hurdles that he pulled gloriously away from the field.

His halfway-stage time of 23 seconds dead was his fastest ever. Hennige of West Germany was runner-up, but John Sherwood, who took third place, returned the same time as the German. Neither, however, had been remotely able to match Hemery's extraordinary feat.

Hemery continued in the steps of Lord Burghley when he won the 400 metres hurdles at the Mexico Olympics in 1968. It was Lord Burghley himself who presented Hemery with his medal.

61

MARY PETERS

Pentathlon gold, 1972

Mary Peters had reached what was, for an athlete, the ripe age of 33 by the time she ebulliently won the Olympic pentathlon in Munich in 1972. It was an immensely popular success by an athlete whose competitive urge had never destroyed her natural generosity and good humour. In an age when winning seemed to justify and dominate everything else, Mary Peters was able to challenge, win and lose with immense good grace and unfailing friendliness. Perhaps it was these qualities which also enabled her to rise above the death and misery which were all about her in Belfast; though even she was glad to escape to the United States on a Churchill scholarship, after her flat had twice been burgled.

Though brought up in Belfast from the age of 11 and always regarded as Northern Irish, Mary Peters came originally from Liverpool, where her father worked in insurance.

In Ulster, Mary Peters attended Portadown College in County Armagh, and was the only girl in the school cricket team. At fourteen, while playing cricket, she was approached by the headmaster, who suggested she try the high jump. Kenneth McClelland, the physical education teacher there, also coached her in sprinting and long jump, and eventually took her to a meeting held at Short and Harland where the celebrated Maeve Kyle suggested she train for the pentathlon.

At that time, Mary Peters had never even heard of shot-putting, but McLelland taught her both this event and the hurdles, and in due course she became Britain's first 50-foot shot-putter, beating the long-standing record of just over 49 feet set by Suzanne Allday. 'But I don't particularly want to be great,' she said, 'I just want to be the best ever in Britain.' An ambition which was duly gratified.

When she was 15, her birthday present from her father (who turned up secretly from Canada to watch her win the pentathlon in Munich) was two tons of sand, so that she could build a jumping pit. At 16, she won the Ulster women's shot-putting championship, and in Tokyo in 1964 she finished an honourable fourth in the pentathlon, selflessly helping Mary Rand to gain her silver medal.

She competed in the 1968 Mexico Olympics, too, but it was in Munich four years later that she truly and triumphantly came into her own. Given intensive weight training by Buster McShane, in whose gymnasium she worked, and fortified by vitamin pills and wheat germ oil, she mastered the Fosbury Flop while in America, thus vastly improving her high jump mark, and by the time it came to Munich she was a formidable all-rounder.

Things, in the pentathlon, had certainly changed since first she competed in the European Championships in Belgrade, 10 years earlier. 'I remember,' she said, 'there was so little public interest that at the end of the event I had to climb over the wall of the stadium in darkness with the team manager, to get home.'

In 1972 in Munich, she put the shot 53 feet 1¾ inches, jumped a formidable 5 feet 11¾ inches, inspired, she said, by the crowd, and returned 13.29 seconds for the 100 metres hurdles. In the long jump and the 200 metres she did well enough to hold on to the lead she had established over the West German competitor, and expert long jumper, Heide Rosendahl. So she finished eight whole places up on her performance in Mexico, her high jump being fully 9¼ inches better.

'When it came to the 200 metres,' she said, 'I knew that if Rosendahl did 23.1 seconds and Pollak (East Germany) 23.9, I would have to do faster than my best of 24.2 to win.' She duly did, to record perhaps the most popular victory in Munich. Her 4,801 points established a new world record.

Mary Peters' power as a shot-putter helped ensure her pentathlon victory at Munich in 1972.

NEIL ADAMS

A world champion at the under-78 kilos mark, as well as a European champion, Neil Adams is one of the outstanding judo men of his era. In the Moscow Olympiad he took a silver medal at the lower weight of under 71 kilos, when he was barely 22. He will certainly be hoping to do better than that in Los Angeles.

So well respected is he in the world of judo that most of his opponents have studied him exhaustively on video; but it does not seem to make any difference to his ability to beat them.

Adams is unusual in his versatility; a refulgent exception to the rule that you excel either at ground-work or at throwing. Adams seems equally good at either, and his elegance on the mat wins the applause of the experts.

His dedication was apparent early; he moved home from Coventry to London at the age of 15 solely because he believed he would have more opportunity for his judo in the capital. He trains for five hours every day, his programme including weights and running, and he is a purist in his sport, deploring those opponents whom he deems 'spoilers and brawlers'.

He would, he thinks, have won a gold medal in Moscow, were it not for the fact that he had to wait five hours before taking part in the final. 'I'd gone flat', he says, 'I just couldn't get going until the very last minute'. Let us hope, as he does, that the wait in Los Angeles will be short.

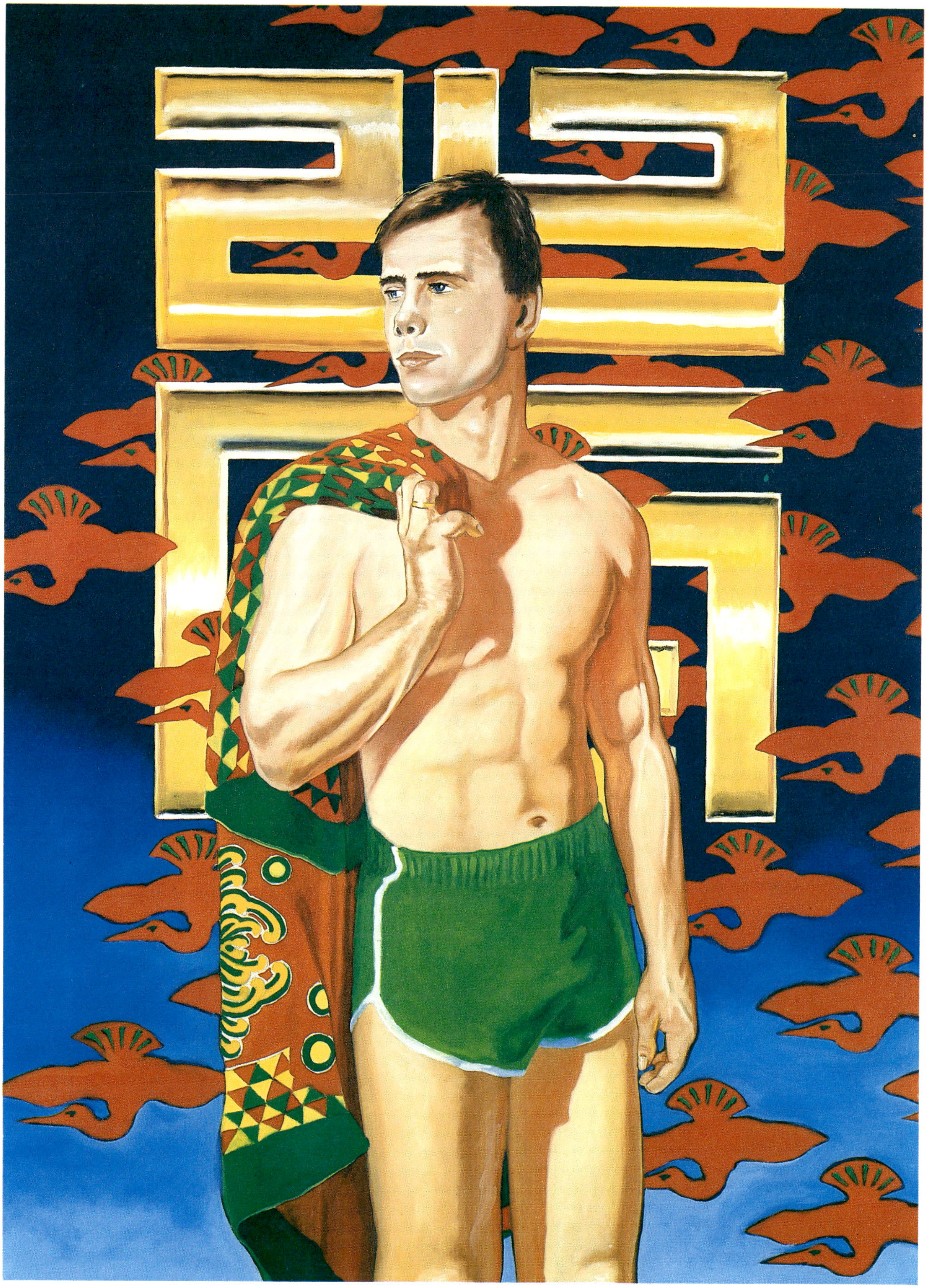

66

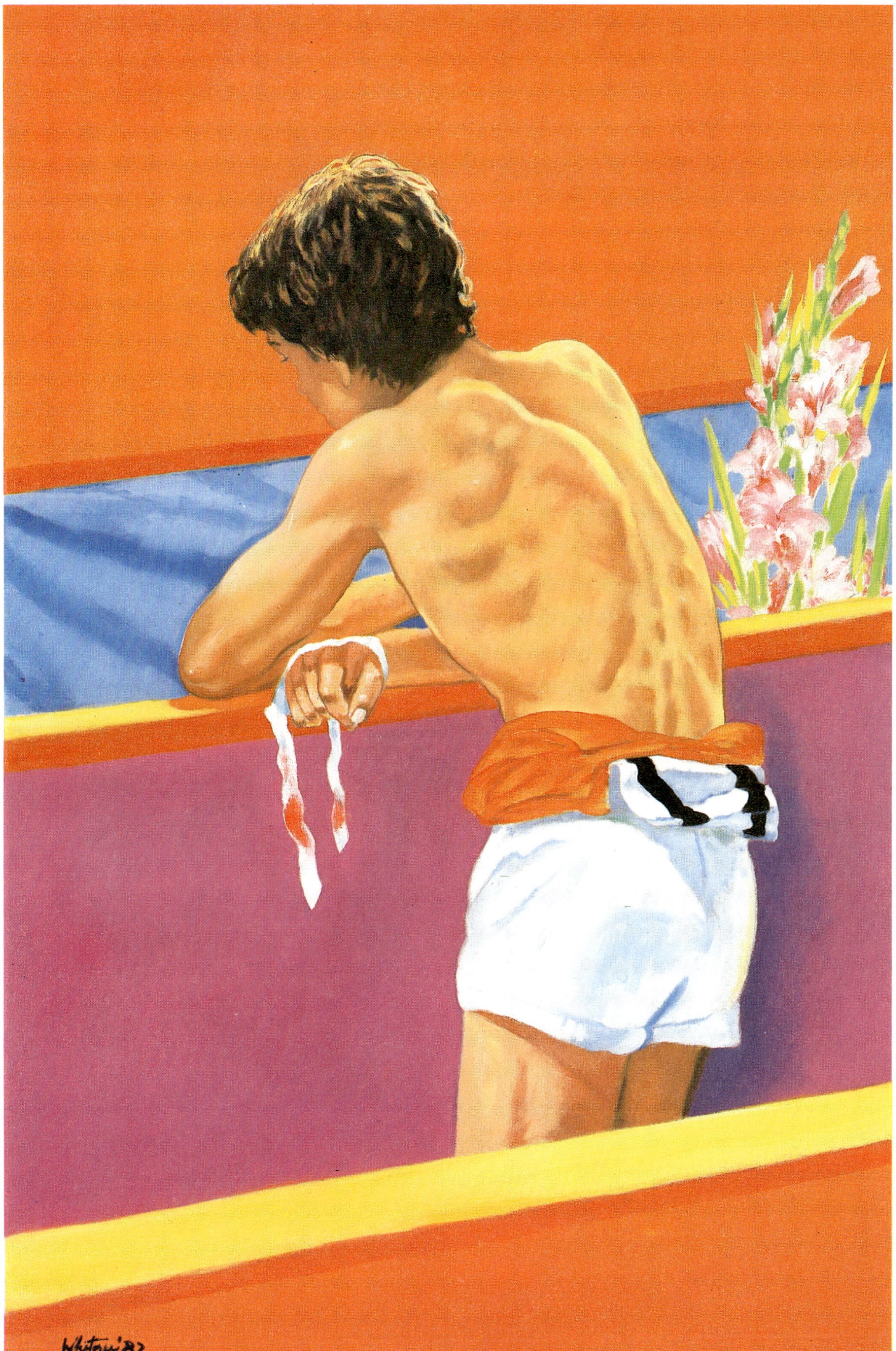
Whitney '83

ANDREW MORRIS

Andrew Morris is the best gymnast Britain has ever produced and he may well finish in the first 36 in Los Angeles. On the surface this seems to say very little. In fact, the achievement of this 22-year-old Welshman from Swansea has, in relative terms, been remarkable. He took a commendable 14th place in the 1983 European Championships in Bulgaria; and he won the British *Daily Mirror* title at Wembley the same year in overwhelming style.

The powerful, elegant, dark-haired Morris is fortunate in having two coaches: Leigh Jones, at his club, and Susan Cheesebrough, his girl friend, formerly an international gymnast of high quality

Morris has even been compared with the celebrated Nadia Comaneci for his attitude and temperament. He has, say his admirers, the same extraordinary ability to cut himself off from everything around him between events, at any championship—the capacity to work out exactly what he needs from each event and, by and large, to get it.

'He's got a computer for a brain,' it's been said. 'This chap has the same quality as Comaneci, this ability to lock himself off.'

His flair for playing the percentages grew very clear when he won his British title at Wembley. In the earlier stages, he outclassed the field on the floor, the pommel horse and the rings, and was able virtually to coast when it came to the parallel and high bars.

Surprisingly, Morris did not take up gymnastics seriously till he was 13, which is late for a leading gymnast. It was Leigh Jones who spotted his talent, took him to Swansea YMCA, from which so many fine gymnasts have emerged, then to the Swansea Gymnastics Club, which Jones founded in a disused church.

Andrew says he enjoys gymnastics for 'the challenge and variety of skill required.' An inverted crucifix on the rings is one of his later and more daring feats.

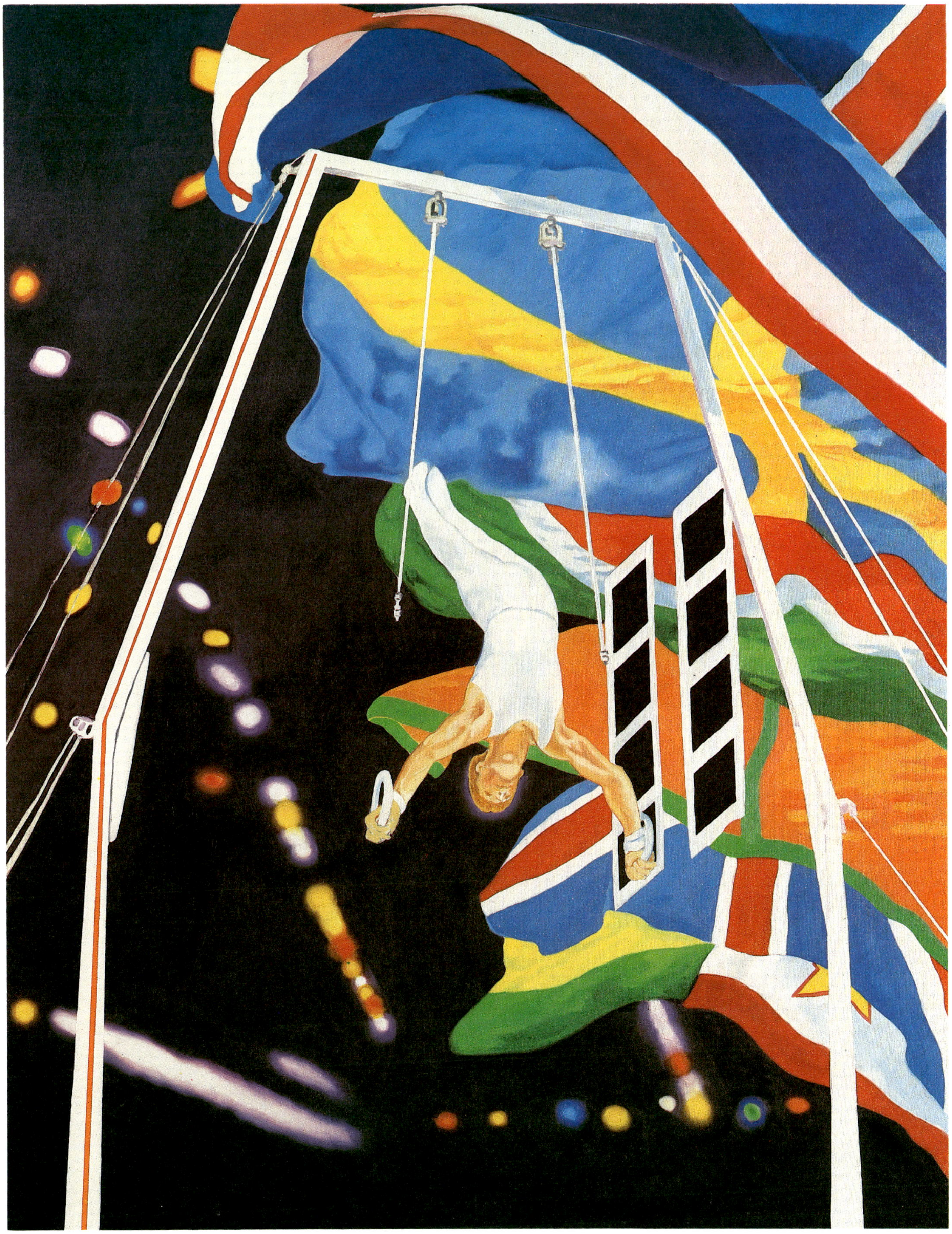

LUCINDA GREEN

Lucinda Green, better and earlier known as Prior-Palmer, has in some sense squared the circle; she has remained beguilingly feminine, while showing an endurance and a commitment which has allowed her to be one of the finest Three Day Event riders of her time. With all this, she has the absolute modesty of the classical Betjeman girl.

This chance in Los Angeles will be a consolation for the fact that she missed the 1980 Moscow Olympics. The British equestrian body decided to bow to the wish of the Government, but Lucinda said that she'd decided not to go, anyway.

Her love of a challenge extends to the kinds of horses she has trained at her Hampshire stables. She prefers a problem; eschews the kind of horse 'that has already succeeded'; likes best of all those which other people have tried to train in vain.

It has nothing, she says, to do with the voice, though everything to do with basic empathy between horse and rider. A period during which, after a throat operation, she was unable to speak convinced her of this.

Lucinda was something of a prodigy, riding Be Fair, her fine chestnut horse, for Britain when she was only 17, in the European Championship, winning Badminton with its fearsome course at 19 and establishing a record of winning it three times more.

She was, she says, 'a typical Thelwell child', going twice a week to the local riding school with her nanny, receiving at the age of nine her first pony, who firmly refused to jump higher than two foot six. 'He needed a good kick, and he taught me to be aggressive, which was later marvellous for Be Fair.'

Aggression, in fact, is not easily visible when she rides; she seems rather to treat her mounts with an affectionate patience. 'If the mind is happy,' she says, 'the body will follow'. Her career seems to have proved as much.

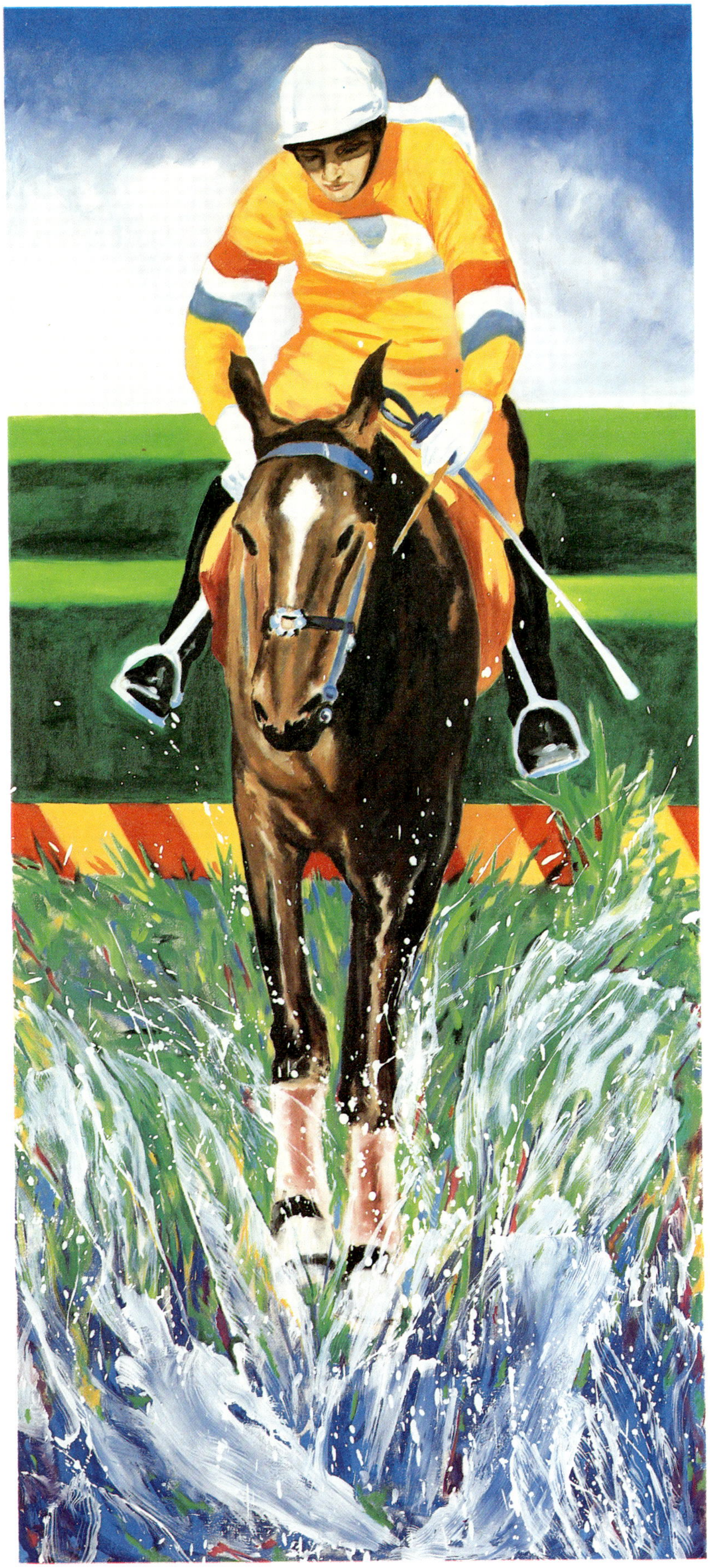

HARRY LLEWELLYN and FOXHUNTER Equestrian gold, 1952

Lieutenant Colonel Harry Llewellyn and his fine 11-year-old horse Foxhunter won Britain's solitary gold medal in the Helsinki Olympiad of 1952.

Born in 1911, Harry Llewellyn was a notable steeplechase jockey long before he became, with Foxhunter, an 'eventer,' winning a bronze medal in the London Olympics of 1948 before his victory in Helsinki. He actually took second place in the Grand National of 1936 on Ego, behind Reynoldstown.

After the war, he quickly became one of Europe's leading show jumpers, first on Kilgeddin, with whom he won the 1946 Victory Cup and the 1947 puissance in Rome. Both Foxhunter and Kilgeddin were ridden in the 1948 Olympics.

In Helsinki, Foxhunter had a bad first round, with no fewer than 16¾ faults, but that was probably because Llewellyn, aware of how much work lay ahead, had deliberately been limiting the amount till then. In the second round, however, after Wilf White on Nizefela had restored Britain's chances with a four-fault second round, Llewellyn took Foxhunter round the course with no faults at all and won the gold medal.

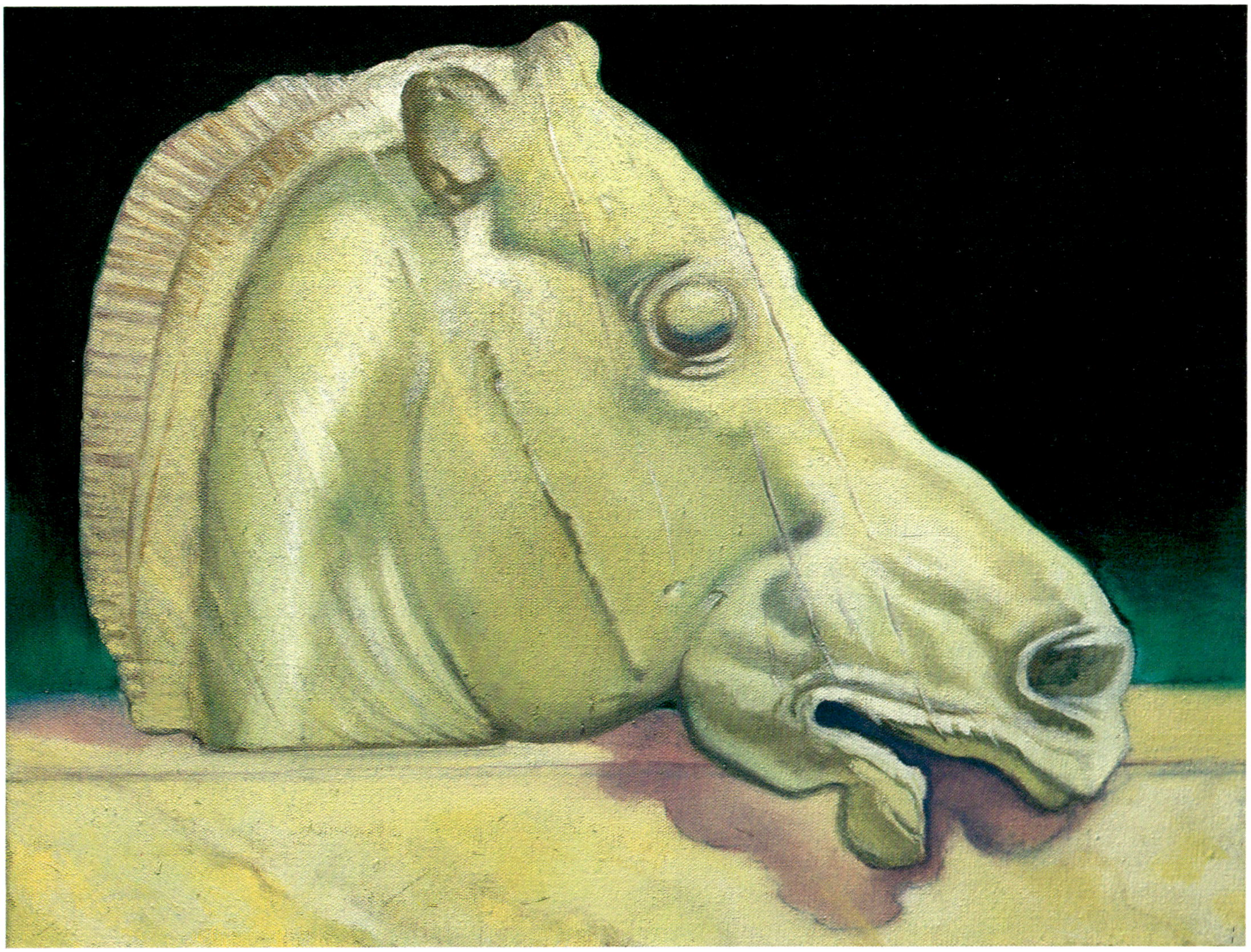

BERYL MITCHELL

In 1982, at the peak of her form as an international sculler, Beryl Mitchell sped downhill on a toboggan, crashed, and fractured her skull. She'd probably be the first to agree that the whole incident somehow encapsulated her character and her career; bold, reckless, unorthodox, even perhaps—in the most beguiling way—perverse. But nowhere near as perverse as the officials who have obstructed, jeopardised and undermined a remarkable career. She tends to lose count of the number of times she's been suspended.

Now in her early 30s, a powerfully athletic, exuberant woman, who has won the television 'Superstars' contest, breaking the *men's* cycling record in the process, she took up sculling as a 15-year-old schoolgirl almost by chance; because ice skating and horseback riding, her preferences, were denied to her. Even then, it was a number of years before she could row single sculls.

Making a springboard of adversity, she has had remarkable successes for an English competitor, pitted against the state-supported Amazons of the Iron Curtain countries. She still remembers the dazed disbelief, the sheer outrage, of the Russian girl she beat to take a silver medal in the world championships of 1981, in Munich. Beryl celebrated by throwing the gold medallist in the water.

In the Moscow Olympics, she came an honourable fifth. She might at her best, she feels, have got a silver medal; 'But they made me row and row and row.'

A Physical Education teacher in Hammersmith, she pays tribute to the 'motivating' influence of her friend and fellow sculler, Lyn Clark: 'An incredible influence on my rowing.'

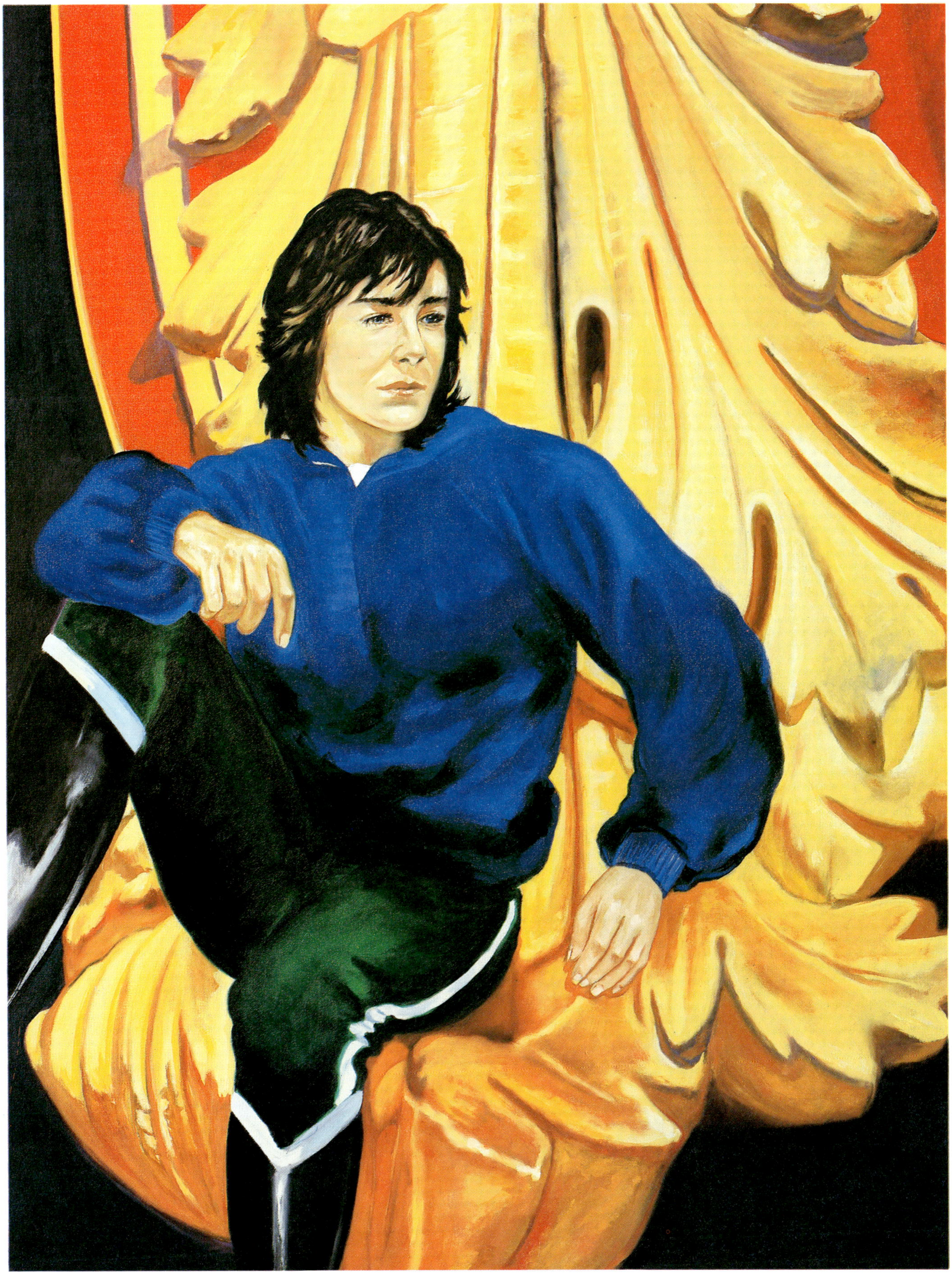

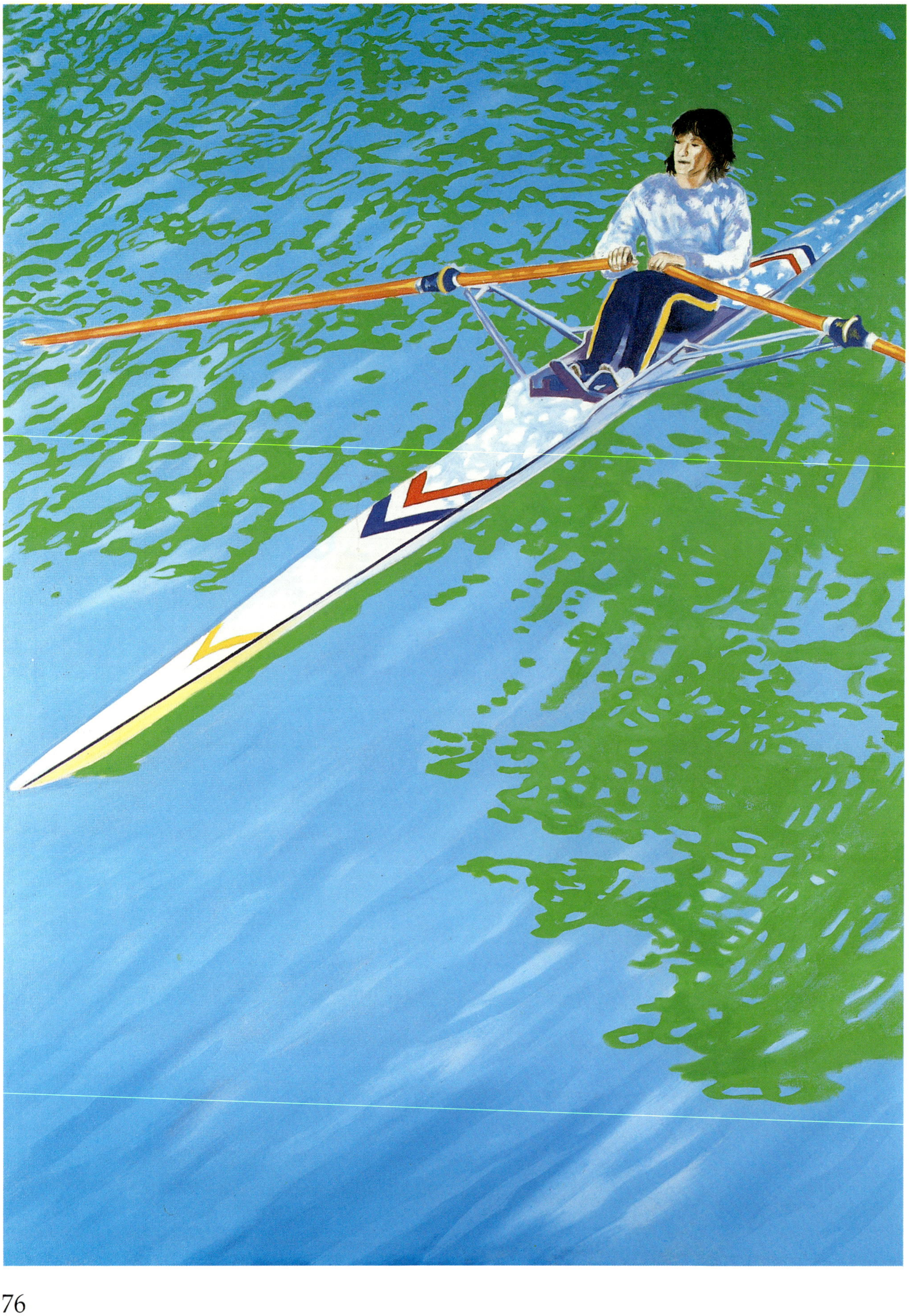

77

CHRIS SNODE

In December, 1983, Chris Snode brought off for the first time the breathtaking feat of a front one-and-a-half somersault with *four* twists. He did it on a 'dry' board in Florida; a testimony not only to his extraordinary gymnastic skills but to his immense courage. A year's work with harness and pulley, coached by Steve McFarland, had been rewarded. Minimal error, Snode knows, would be punished by painful injury. 'It took me three hours,' he admitted, 'to get psyched up for the attempt, for something no one has ever tried before.'

So the once unthinkable, the once unattainable, becomes the logical quest of the Olympic athlete, as he strives to establish and to hold – for just long enough – that edge which alone will gain him a gold medal in his event. In running, we have the four-minute mile, now commonplace. In diving, we now have the four twists.

Chris Snode equalled Brian Phelps' enviable record in Brisbane in the 1982 Commonwealth Games when he took both diving titles – the springboard and the highboard – at the age of 23. This was substantial consolation for the Hornchurch diver for his disappointment in the Moscow Olympics, when he finished only sixth, and in the subsequent European championships, when he could come no higher than fifth.

Inconsistency was the charge levelled against him then, for it was well known that, at his gymnastic, daring best, he was the equal of any diver in the world. But the triumphs in Brisbane suggested that he might well have overcome that fault at last. If so, then his chances of a medal in Los Angeles must be real.

In 1976, when a mere 17-year-old, the Essex boy arrived in Gainsville on a swimming scholarship at the University of Florida, sleeping on that sunlit campus with a Union Jack over his bed, and on a Union Jack pillow. He was, he explained, very patriotic.

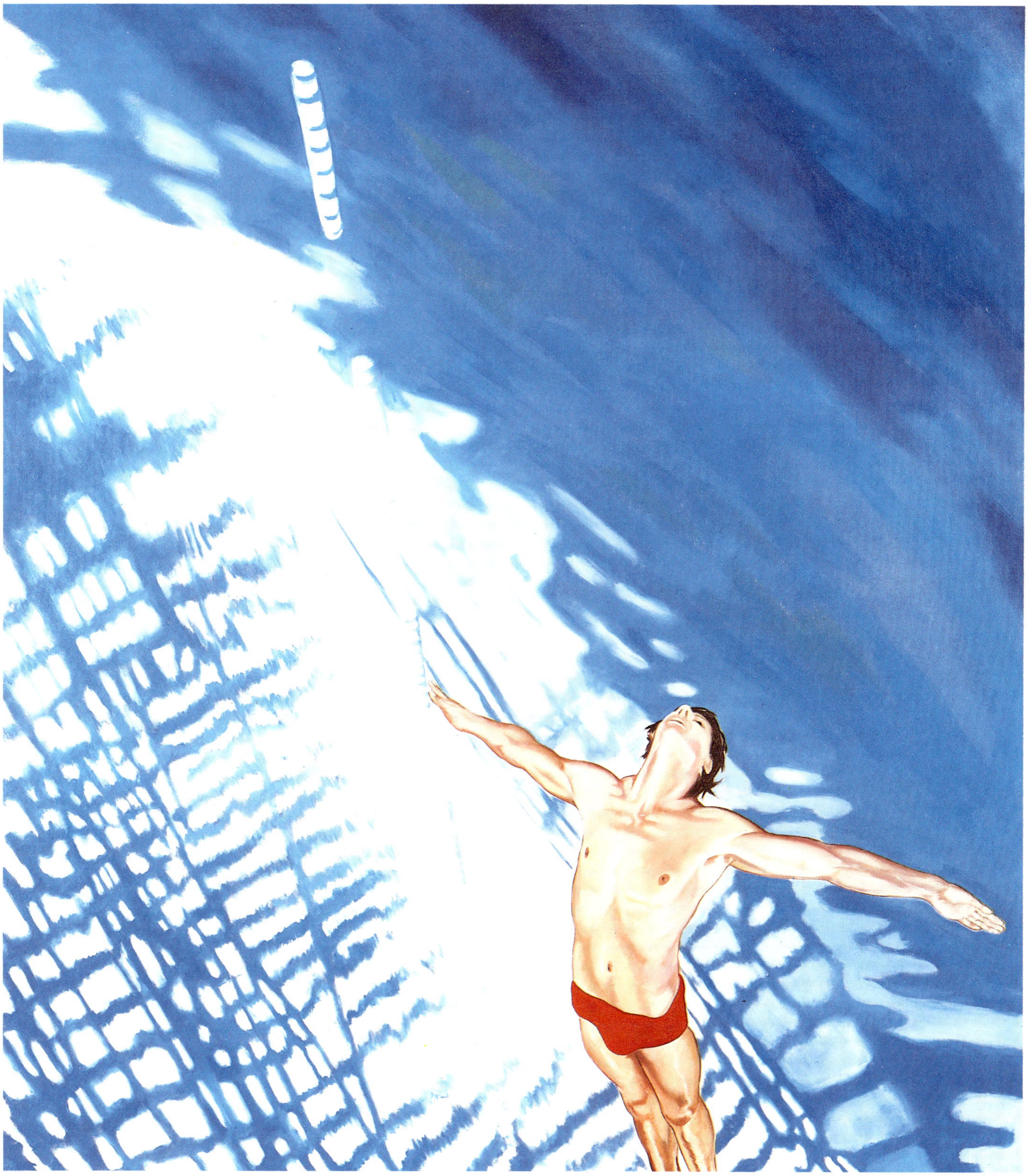

Enormously hard work under an able coach, John Rasch, who died, sadly and suddenly, during the 1976 Montreal Olympics, laid the basis of Snode's achievements. In Gainsville, his day of training would begin at six in the morning in the gym or on the trampoline. Then on to three-quarters of an hour's basic diving, with weight training, running and, of course, diving itself, in the crowded afternoon.

After taking both diving medals in the Edmonton Commonwealth Games, he proved his prowess the following year with a famous victory in the World Cup three metres event in Woodlands, Texas, when he beat the formidable American, Phil Boggs.

The idea that the Moscow Olympics could elude him because Britain might withdraw her athletes on political grounds he 'didn't understand' depressed him dreadfully. He thought he had a fine chance of winning the three metres gold medal. He went, and he didn't win; but 1982 was perhaps the watershed. He added three new dives to his repertoire, including the backward two-and-a-half somersault pike, and his victory over a brilliant field in the Martini European Diving Cup at Crystal Palace was the prelude to his victories in Brisbane.

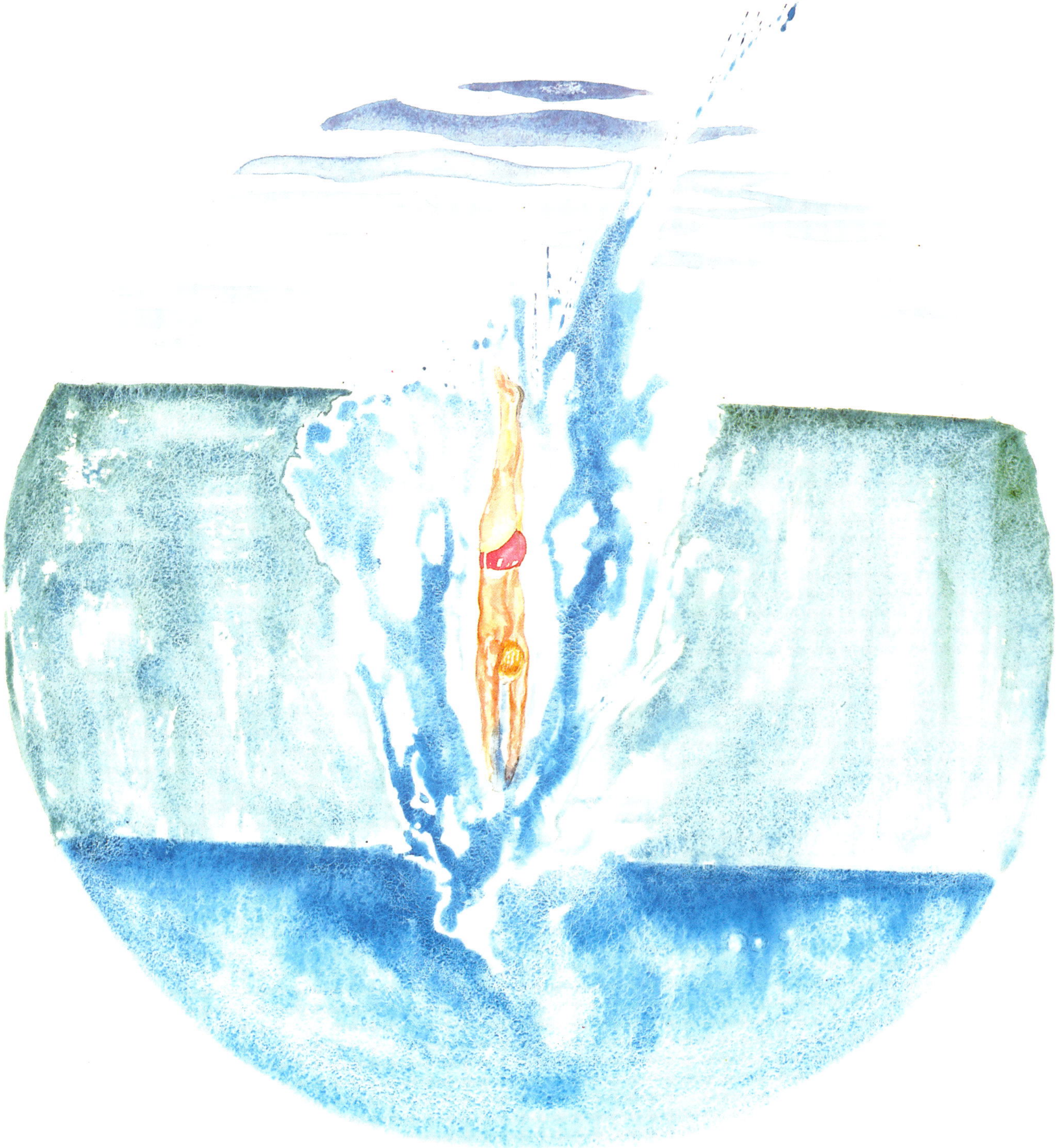

PHIL HUBBLE

Phil Hubble was 20 years old when, in the Moscow Olympics, he surpassed himself to win the silver medal in the gruelling 200 metres butterfly race. In these precocious days 24 may be a ripe old age for a swimmer, but it also means that those who can manage to stay the course for so long bring to their event an extra experience, a battle hardness if you will, which can serve them well. Hubble, therefore, could well be a force again in the 1984 games in Los Angeles, even though opponents will be better aware of him now.

A Slough man, never afraid to speak his mind when he feels that someone, or some official, has blundered, Hubble ironically took the Olympic silver with a time that was not as good as the Commonwealth record he had set the same morning. Sergey Fesenko, his Russian conqueror in the final, had been just ahead of him, as he was destined to be later that day. Fesenko was the first Russian male swimmer ever to win an Olympic gold medal.

Hubble is a splendid fighter who never gives up, and this was shown abundantly in that Moscow final. He was no better than sixth after 50 metres, and at 100 metres had still not improved his position. He had made up two places at the start of the last lap, and then, in his own words, 'managed to get a good kick into the start of that lap.' This was putting it mildly and modestly. Away he went for a final time of 2 minutes 1.20 seconds, which was better than anybody but Fesenko, who clocked 1.59.16.

An honest and objective self-analyst, Hubble admitted afterwards that he was more nervous in the final than in the morning's preliminary and, by contrast with that morning, 'went too hard on the first 100 metres and it hurt a bit.' He might, as he said, have broken two minutes had he swum as well and in as relaxed a state as he had in the heat, but the silver medal was, as he said, 'great'. And he is still with us.

83

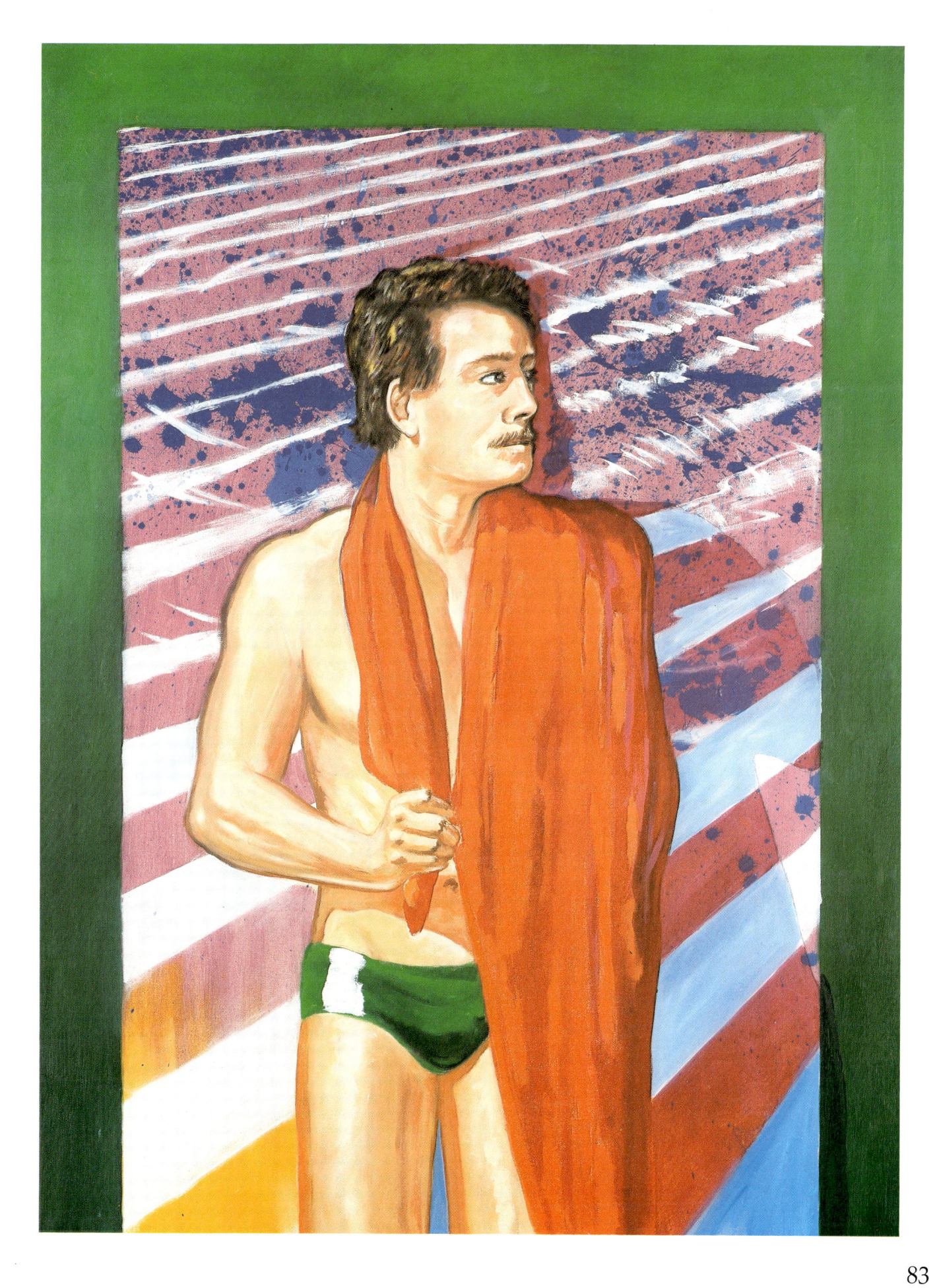

ADRIAN MOORHOUSE

'Over the last 15 metres, I kept saying to myself, "You've got to win for the Queen." She gave me inspiration.' So spoke Adrian Moorhouse, the splendid, 19-year-old breaststroke swimmer from Bingley, Yorkshire, when he won a gold medal for England in the final of the Commonwealth Games 100 metres event, in Brisbane. Beating the Canadian world record holder Vic Davis in his triumphant final burst, he was only 0.4 seconds outside the world record himself, finishing in a time of 1 minute 2.93 seconds, which was itself a British and Games record.

It was characteristic of Moorhouse's approach to swimming that he should say modestly afterwards, 'At the World Championships in Ecuador I finished fourth, but knew I could go faster if I could only get my dive and my turn right. I haven't had much chance to practise, but I managed to improve the dive a bit, although the turn was still not very great.'

Abundant time to practise, and to make himself a leading challenger for the gold in Los Angeles, in the steps of Wilkie and Goodhew, lay ahead of him. He was given a four-year scholarship in California at Berkeley. From Bingley to Berkeley was a sharp transition, but one which Moorhouse seemed well capable of making.

As a 17-year-old, he had already done great things. Six feet tall, splendidly built, he had shown his formidable capacity early in 1981 at the Speedomeet in Amersfoort. There, he surprised the swimming world by beating two of the best Russian breaststrokers—Zhulpa, the Olympic 200 metres champion, being one of them. Knocking two seconds off his previous best time, and moving thus into the top 10 in the world, he won the 100 metres in 1 minute 5.12 seconds.

Better things still lay ahead. Moorhouse went to Moscow to train with the Soviet swimmers. Back in England, his mother informed us that he got up at 5

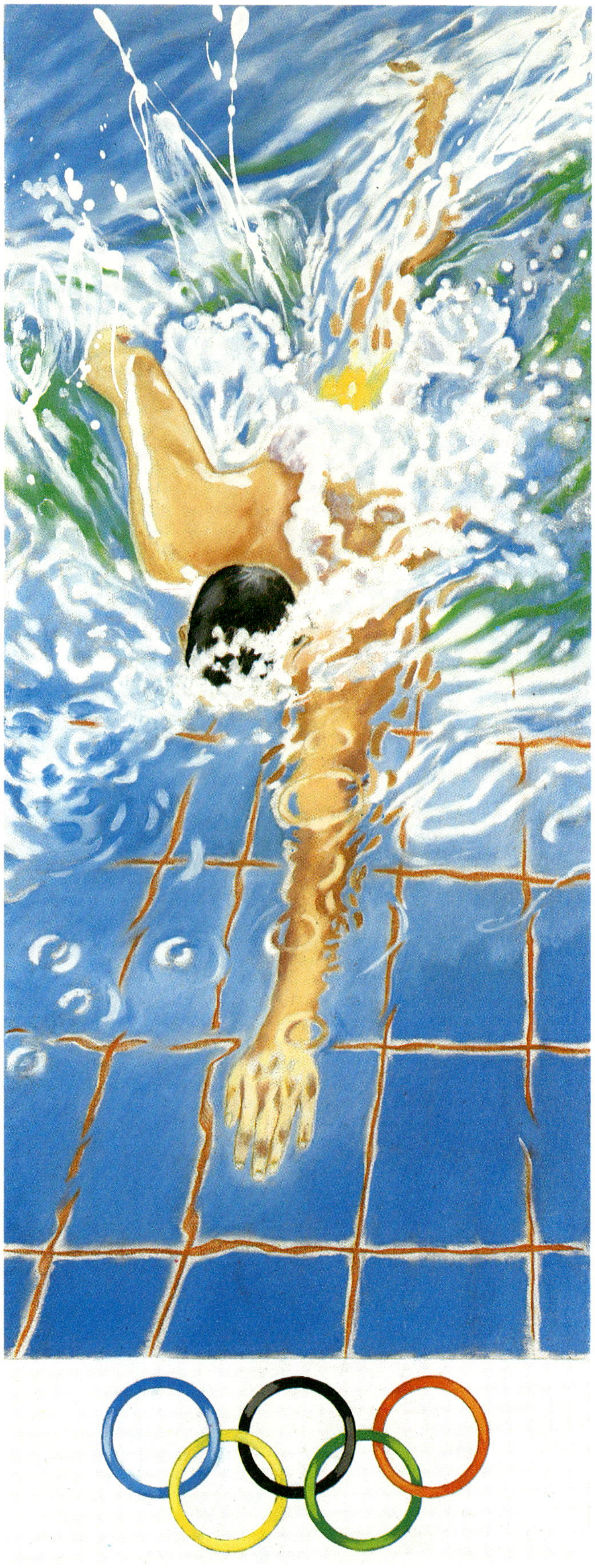

o'clock in the morning every day except Sundays and Tuesdays, so that he could swim for an hour-and-a-half in the Leeds international pool, before turning up at Bingley Grammar School for lessons. He trains for a further two hours every evening, said his mother.

In September 1981, at the European Swimming Championships in Yugoslavia, Moorhouse took the bronze medal in the 200 metres. Experts felt that lack of experience alone may have cost him the silver. His time of 2 minutes 18.4 seconds was a new English record. 'I thought of breaking the English record,' he said, 'but it really was a dream to boost myself. I didn't think I could get close to Zhulpa (the Olympic champion) especially after I put everything into my heat this morning. But knocking four seconds off my best time and getting a medal is fantastic.'

In the subsequent European Championships, in Rome, Moorhouse did get a silver, and very nearly a gold, in the 100 metres breaststroke. Zhulpa this time beat him by the merest margin of 5/100ths of a second. 'I thought I'd won it,' said Moorhouse, 'even though I misjudged my finish slightly. Then I saw two go up against my name, and realised Zhulpa had come through on the outside.'

Let us hope that 'one' goes up in Los Angeles.

HENRY TAYLOR — 400 and 1,500 metres freestyle gold, 1908

The peak of Henry Taylor's career was the 1908 London Olympics, where he won no fewer than three gold medals for swimming. He began life as an orphan, and concluded it as a pool attendant at his local Chadderton baths, having long since lost the money (raised from pawning all his silver cups) to run a public house.

Born in 1885 in Oldham, Lancashire, Taylor adored swimming, and was an early example of a British swimmer rising to success above bleak circumstances. He swam anywhere he could, usually in canals and streams during his lunch hour, or in the evenings. He could afford to go to the local baths only on so-called 'dirty water' days, when the price was cheaper.

The stroke he swam was not the crawl but the trudgeon. At the London Olympiad, he won the 400 metres in a world record time of 5 minutes 36.8 seconds, beating Frank Beaurepaire of Australia by fully 7.4 seconds. In the final of the 1,500 metres, he came 2.8 seconds ahead of Britain's Sydney Battersby, in 22 minutes 48.4 seconds, a new world record for the distance. A third gold medal came in the 4 × 200 metres freestyle relay, Britain beating Hungary into second place.

He competed less successfully in the subsequent Olympic Games in Stockholm, retiring in the semi-finals of the 1,500 metres, losing in the semi-finals of the 400 metres, but getting a bronze in the relay. He swam in the last of his 15 British Championships at the age of 35: it was a five mile race in the Thames.

Henry Taylor, seen here with his trainer, won two gold medals in the 1908 Olympic Games in London.

LUCY MORTON — 200 metres breaststroke gold, 1924

Lucy Morton (right) raced against Constance Jeans (left) in the Ladies Long Distance Swimming Championship, held in London in 1920.

Lucy Morton fully deserved the gold medal she won for Britain in the 200 metres breaststroke in Paris in 1924—the last swimming gold medal Britain would win for 32 years.

Born at Knutsford, Cheshire, in 1898, she would surely have won the title in 1916 had it not been for the war. She was the world record holder at the time. Four years later in Antwerp, when the Olympic Games were resumed, her event was not included in the programme. In 1924, in Paris, her luck at last turned. A champion backstroke as well as a breaststroke swimmer, in the overarm and frog kick style, she was not the favourite in Paris, going there as second string to Irene Gilbert, who then held the world record for the distance. But Miss Gilbert fell ill, and the Dutch girl, Marie Baron, who swam the fastest qualifying time, was disqualified for a faulty turn.

Agnes Geraghty of the United States took the lead in the final and was still ahead at 150 metres. Lucy Morton then made her effort, and forged ahead of her to win the race in a time of 3 minutes 33.2 seconds. Irene Gilbert did swim the race, but was 17.6 seconds outside her own world record, which at that time was far better than Miss Morton's winning Olympic time.

Later, as Mrs Heaton, Miss Morton became a teacher of swimming and an official of the sport.

JUDY GRINHAM 100 metres backstroke gold, 1956

Buoyant, modest and engaging, quite untouched by the pressures and rigours which would turn so many young swimmers into creatures old before their time, Judy Grinham was not only an unexpected champion, but a vastly popular one; a champion who seemed to have stepped from the anachronistic pages of some schoolgirl's annual.

When she won, by a touch, the 100 metres backstroke final at the Melbourne Olympic Games of 1956, it was

When Judy Grinham (right) won the 100 metres backstroke gold in the Melbourne Olympics, her friend Margaret Edwards (left) won the bronze.

the first gold swimming medal Britain had taken since Lucy Morton won the 200 metres breaststroke final in the Paris Games of 1924.

17 years old, Miss Grinham had to overcome a severe attack of nerves before the race, and she made, inevitably, a poor beginning, even though she had previously set a new Olympic record of 1 minute 13.1 seconds in the heats. Her English rival, Margaret Edwards, had then returned 1 minute 13 seconds.

For the first 50 metres of the final, Judy's fear that she would not be able

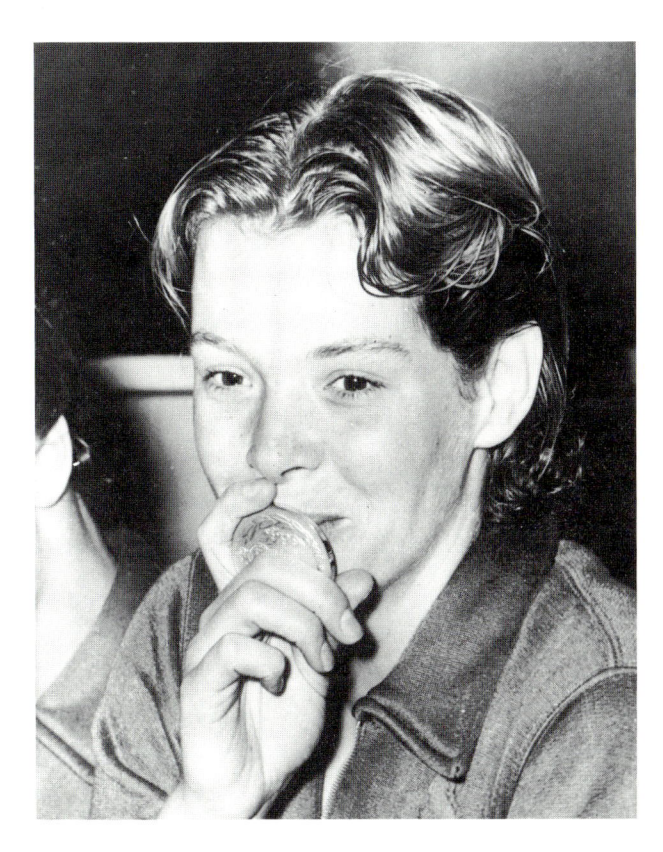

Judy Grinham (right) is welcomed by her parents (below) on her victorious return from the Melbourne Olympics.

to swim a stroke seemed almost justified. She was only in fifth place at the turn, but then the penny dropped. With a stupendous spurt, Judy made up ground so well that with 10 metres left she had drawn level with the leader, the blonde American, Carin Cone. At the finish, she touched just ahead of her, although they were both given the same Olympic record time of 1 minute 12.9 seconds. Margaret Edwards finished an impressive third in 1 minute 13.1 seconds, with a third English girl, Julie Hoyle, in sixth place.

The shy, modest, endearing Miss Grinham, who had twice been turned down by the Hampstead swimming club which she ultimately joined, went on to win the Commonwealth Games 110 yards backstroke event at Cardiff two years later in a world record time of 1 minute 11.9 seconds. To this, later that year, she added the European 100 metres title, in Budapest. She also played a major part, swimming a fine first leg, in England's Commonwealth Games victory in the 110 yards medley relay, beating a powerful Australian team anchored by the formidable Dawn Fraser.

Judy retired in March 1959 at the age of 20, one of the finest swimmers of her time.

The 1958 world-record holders for the women's medley team race pose together – from front to back: Diana Wilkinson, Judy Grinham, Christine Godsen and Anita Lonsbrough.

ANITA LONSBROUGH 200 metres breaststroke gold, 1960

A surprisingly late developer as a breaststroke swimmer, Anita Lonsbrough, from Huddersfield in Yorkshire, won a splendidly judged victory in the final of the 200 metres breaststroke in the Rome Olympics of 1960. She relied on her belief that if she attacked the favourite, Wiltrud Urselmann of Germany, in the later stages of the race, the German might crack.

Coolness prevailed. Being the favourite had obviously disturbed Urselmann, whereas Lonsbrough was so composed that she even varnished her nails before she set off for the race.

19 years old at the time, she had

Anita Lonsbrough swam freestyle before concentrating on the breaststroke with which she beat the world. She returned to freestyle again after her Olympic victory and performed well in the individual medley in Tokyo in 1964.

taken up breaststroke swimming only three years earlier, having been a freestyle swimmer of no great renown. She swam for Great Britain for the first time in May 1958, and a couple of months later she won the Commonwealth Games gold medal for the 220 yards breaststroke in Cardiff. She followed that, a month later, with second place in the 200 metres at the European Championships.

As Anita expected, Urselmann made a very fast start. She led for the first length, with Anita just behind her, but by the third length the Yorkshire girl was pressing her hard, and in the final lap she drew level with her for the first time. With an immense last effort Anita won by half a second in a world record time of 2 minutes 49.5 seconds. It was the only world record set in the women's individual events.

Two years later, despite having lost time through illness, Anita defied cold, damp conditions to win the European 200 metres title in Leipzig. In the subsequent Commonwealth Games, she not only kept her 200 metres title but annexed the gold medals for the 110 metres breaststroke and the 440 yards individual medley. That was in Perth, Australia.

Having proved herself the finest breaststroke swimmer in the world, she became a freestyler again, and came seventh in the individual medley final of the 1964 Tokyo Olympics.

Anita Lonsbrough smiles with delight after winning the Olympic 200 metres breaststroke gold in Rome in 1960.

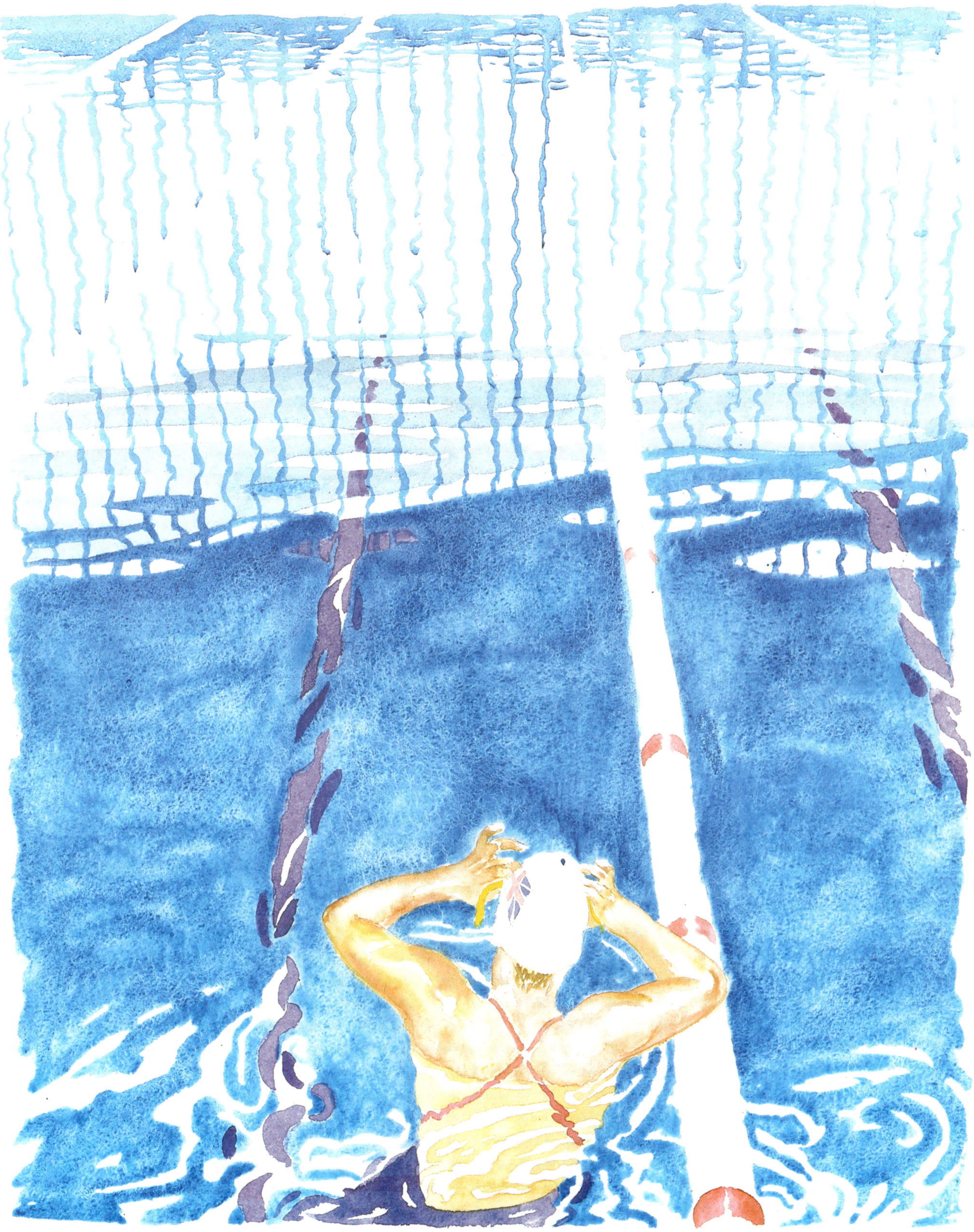

DAVID WILKIE — 200 metres breaststroke gold, 1976

The extent of David Wilkie's achievement in winning the Olympic gold medal for the 200 metres breaststroke event in 1976 in Montreal was one of . . . 68 years. Not since the resilient Taylor, with his trudgeon stroke, in the London Games of 1908, had any male Briton won an Olympic swimming final.

Certainly Wilkie, by the time the race began, had to be the favourite. He had not lost over the distance to his chief rivals for three years, and his enormous natural talent was allied to a highly competitive approach to his sport. It must be said, and he himself said it, that living and training at an American university played a major part in his success. 'If I'd stayed in the United Kingdom,' he said, after his victory, 'I would have given up swimming by now. There are so many problems to overcome back home, not the least of which is finding bath space in which to train at reasonable hours. I am really grateful to America for having given me the chance to win this gold.'

The son of a Scottish expatriate who eventually retired to Aberdeen—where Wilkie had his post-Olympic reception—it was in Sri Lanka (then called Ceylon) that the basis of his success was built. There, Wilkie learned to swim as a child, revelling in the climate, the freedom and the privi-

David Wilkie surges powerfully through the water on his way to win the 200 metres breaststroke gold in 1976.

leged life, and suffering when he was packed off to school at Daniel Stewart College in Edinburgh. Only in the summer holidays could he go back to his beloved Sri Lanka. Those boarding school years he describes as 'sheer hell', and he reacted bitterly against them. The swimming coaches could see the enormous potential of a boy who had been gambolling in the water almost since infancy; but he did everything he could to avoid swimming training.

Even as late as 1972, when he surprisingly won a silver medal at the Munich Olympics in the 200 metres breaststroke, his Edinburgh coach Frank Thomas could say, 'He was always a determined swimmer and a good trainer in the water, but he wouldn't always get to the water. It's my belief still that David had the poorest background of all eight finalists in his event in Munich.'

But perhaps the 6-foot-1-inch Wilkie, in his bathing cap and goggles, had the greatest natural talent.

He was only 18 at the time, and it was clear that he possessed what in football is known as 'the big match temperament.' Miami University was one of the several American colleges that approached him with scholarship offers. They paid for his flight to Florida, and he settled there, training, in the agreeable climate, much harder than ever before. He also became in-

David Wilkie stands proudly displaying his medals.

creasingly competitive. 'I don't believe,' he said, 'in the gentleman's attitude you find in British sport. You know: "it's not the winning that's so important, it's the taking part." You don't want to spend four hours a day training in a pool and then go to a race to get beaten by somebody else. You want to damn well win.'

As the 1976 Montreal Olympics approached, so his duel with the considerably shorter American breaststroker, John Hencken, to whom he scarcely ever spoke, became more and more intense. It was Hencken who took the gold in the Munich Olympics when

Wilkie, surprisingly, took the silver. 'You could say,' said Wilkie, before the Montreal swimming tournament, 'that the only thing we have in common is that we don't speak to each other. . . . In both races, Hencken will go out hard and fast. If my strokes are going well, I don't worry. He'll be going, I'll be chasing.'

The previous year, in the newly inaugurated world swimming championships in Cali, Wilkie had taken both the 100 and the 200 metres breaststroke events. Now, in Montreal, although he broke the world record in the 100 metres final, it was John Hencken who beat him once again, to take the gold. Wilkie swam a time of 1 minute 3.43 seconds and was barely a stroke behind.

But in his better event, the 200 metres, he took his revenge—and the gold. Knocking an astonishing eight-and-a-half seconds off his Munich time, he won in 2 minutes 15.11 seconds, more than a couple of seconds ahead of Hencken who, like Wilkie, beat the world record. As they climbed out of the pool, Wilkie ruffled Hencken's hair and said, 'Thanks, John, it's been a good four years.'

'It has been, David,' said Hencken.

Gold medallists David Wilkie and Duncan Goodhew train together in 1980.

DUNCAN GOODHEW 100 metres breaststroke gold, 1980

When Duncan Goodhew was 10 years old, he fell out of a tree. The cruel consequence of this was that he lost all his hair, which exposed him to spiteful taunting at school. His plight was made worse by the fact that he was dyslexic. 'At first,' he said, 'my hair only came out in tufts. Then I developed a monk's bald pate, and one day in the gymnasium, I got up off the mat, and my hair was still there—all of it. That's a cruel age, especially when you're at boarding school. There I was, bald and unable to write or spell. I was just a stupid oddity.' The poor child couldn't even swim without discomfort, as the lack of any lashes allowed the chlorine to get painfully into his eyes. 'Now,' he said much later, 'I can see that the experience was an important step for me. It helped form my character, made me far more competitive. Life had done me badly, and I had to settle the score.' You might say that he settled it finally and resoundingly when, in the steps—or strokes—of David Wilkie, he won the 1980 gold medal in Moscow for the 100 metres breaststroke race—the medal that had eluded Wilkie in Montreal.

Tony Roberts, who was the swimming coach at Windlesham House

Duncan Goodhew makes a flying start in the 100 metres breaststroke.

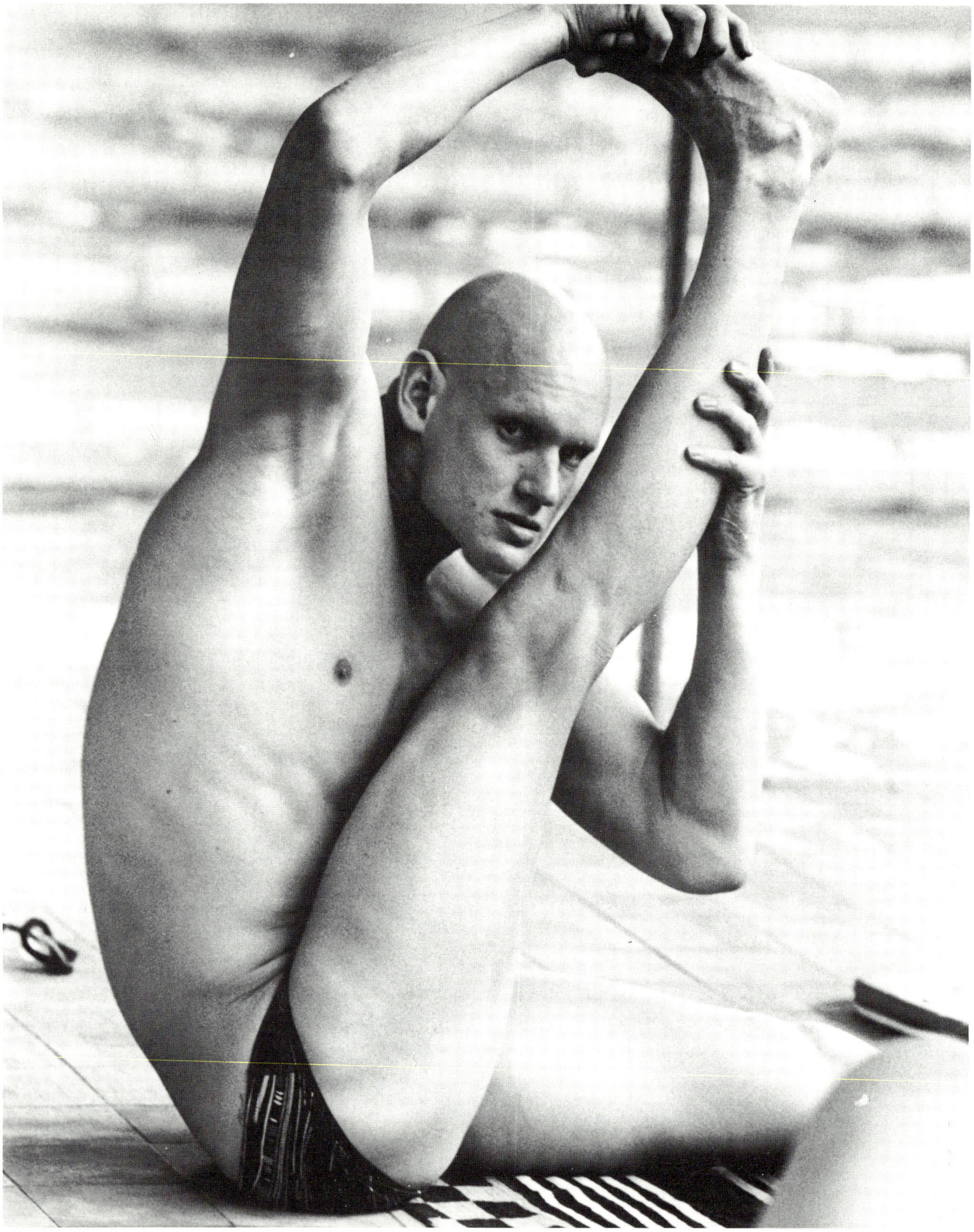

School, needed only three-quarters of an hour to teach Goodhew how to breaststroke a couple of lengths. When he was 12, the school was so impressed that it sent him to the nearby Worthing Swimming Club for special lessons. The following year, a leading coach, John Hogg, said Goodhew had the capacity to be a world champion. And so to Millfield School in Somerset, where many potential champions are nurtured.

Like David Wilkie, Goodhew found his way to the United States with a college swimming scholarship, though he did not settle there quite so snugly. In North Carolina, the swimming coach, Don Easterling, promised that he would take the silver spoon out of Goodhew's mouth. Goodhew even pretended that he smoked and drank, so reluctant was he to submit himself to the training regimen. Easterling called him 'the chrome domed boozer,' but persevered. 'I was stubborn and lazy,' admitted Goodhew, 'and to them, a strange Englishman. But America taught me about winning. Their society is geared to it, from school up: competing and winning. Everything I am now is here in Britain, but my attitude is still American. . . . In sport, it's essential to be a bad loser. Okay, so it's sad, but that's the price you have to pay to be at the top.'

In Moscow, wearing the tweed cap of his adored late father, an RAF officer, Goodhew swam on to the final. The degree of his commitment to winning may be seen from what happened earlier in 1980, when he lost by a fractional margin to the Russian, Arsen Miskarov. He purposely did not warm up after his swim so he would feel ill, as indeed he did, the next morning.

Before the final, he forgot that in Moscow there are three preliminary whistles, rather than two. He had already lain down and imagined the whole race, stroke by stroke, ending in his own victory. 'End of the pool, end of the pool,' he kept saying to himself, up on the block. 'I'm oblivious to the starter calling me down three times, I don't even *hear* him. An official tugs at my arm. I'm vaguely aware of flicking her away. It's an interference; I'm locked into that letter T.' The T junction made, that is to say, by his own lane and the far wall.

He won, of course. 'You can't run before you can crawl,' he said, the following year. 'The very few sportsmen who achieve excellence quickly fall just as quickly. The only effective method of altering an athlete's psyche is probably brainwashing, but my most valued thing is the approach I built to get my ability out of me. Sport, in a sense, is its own religion.' A far cry indeed from the time when 'I used to be known as Duncan the Dunce, and told to sit in a corner and shut up, just because I found it difficult to read.'

Unlike so many swimmers, young and precocious, Goodhew was a 23-year-old man when he won his gold medal. After 50 metres, Goodhew was 0.02 seconds behind Russia's Federowski, but in the second length he surged past both him and his compatriot, Miskarov, to win by a metre, in 1 minute 3.34 seconds. 'I didn't know I was second at the turn,' he said, 'and I won't believe I've won until I hold that medal in my hand. I let my mind wander three-quarters of the way down the first length, and came out of the turn too hard, and had to ease a bit on the way back.'

So the years of effort and isolation had borne fruit. 'I like company,' Goodhew said, later that year, 'but the trouble is, swimmers live a horrible one-track life, and they're so bloody bad tempered all the time that the only people who will put up with them are other swimmers.'

Now he had swum his way free.

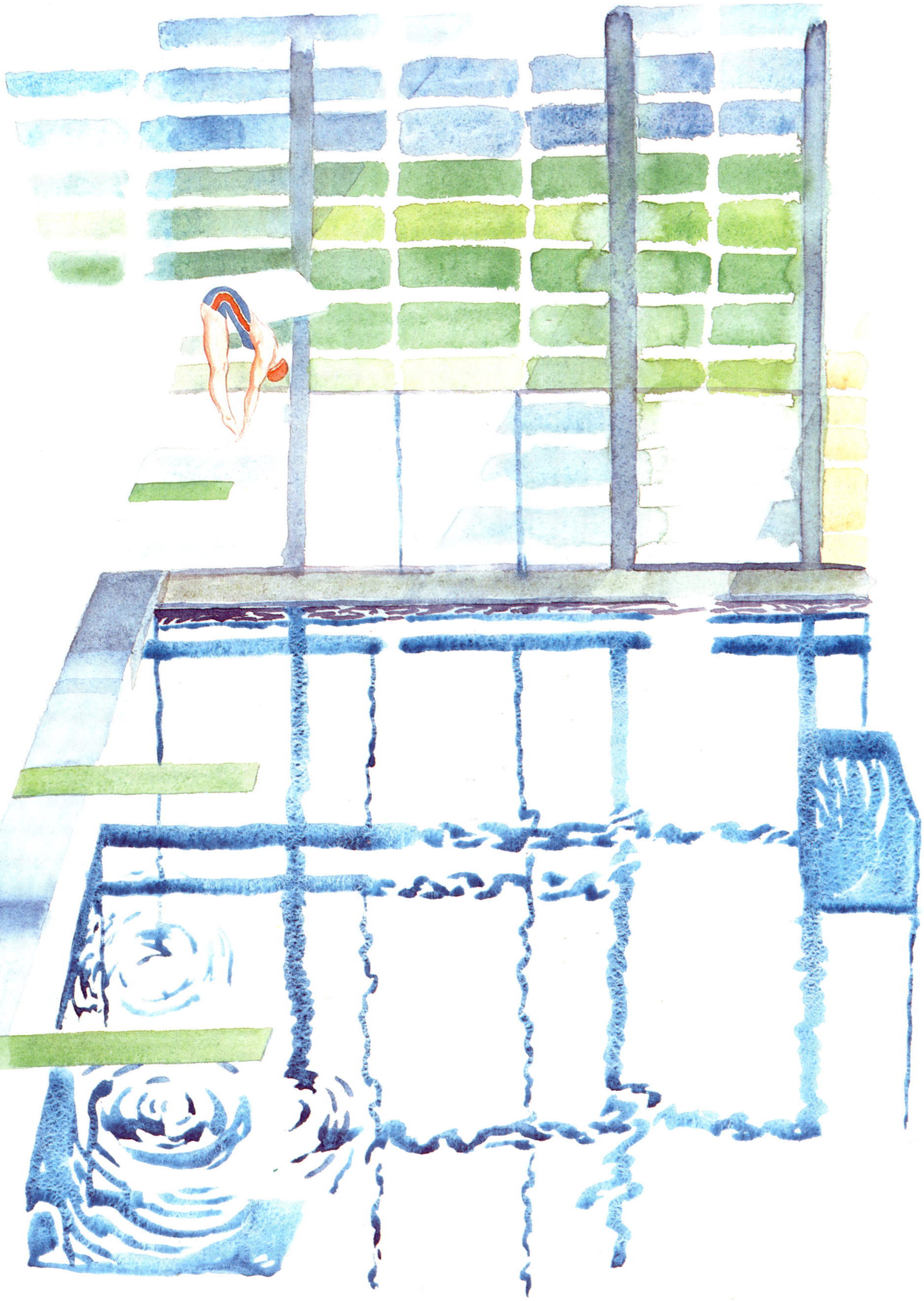

104

105

TORVILL and DEAN

If there is a distinguishing quality about Jayne Torvill and Christopher Dean, beyond their courage, grace, athleticisim and flair, it must surely be their daring. Who else, with the Olympic gold medal virtually in their grasp after a string of world championships, would take such a leap into the void, abandon routines which were in themselves immensely bold and innovatory, for a new one which even the most famous of contemporary skaters felt excessive?

Plainly Dean and Torvill are keen to push the frontiers of a once genteel event to the uttermost limits. They are no mere skaters, but acrobats and gymnasts of the ice. That they should take *Barnum* as their circus theme was indicative and proper; but now they have gone even beyond *Barnum*, into new realms of controversial experiment.

Cousins, studying and studying the new *Bolero* routine on tape, analysing its extraordinary gyrations and novelties, pronounced it 'much more controversial than *Barnum*. It's clever, it's wonderful, it's very imaginative, and no one else would ever skate like this.' But he also felt that Torvill and Dean were sailing awfully close to the wind, that in a routine so brazenly unusual, they ran the risk of being damned for a single fault, a single fall—which, no doubt, is one of the reasons that inspired them to do what they did, to renounce the safer course which would lead, almost automatically, to a gold medal, and gamble with what was surely their dearest ambition. For an Olympic tournament comes much more rarely than a world title. At all events, they won in Sarajevo.

Jayne Torvill and Christopher Dean come from Nottingham, a city which has looked after them well with generous grants. Jayne, unlike Chris, did not begin as an ice dancer. She was a figure skater, both solo and as one of a pair. At 12 years old, coached by Thelma Perry, she won the British junior pairs title with Michael

107

Hutchinson. By contrast, Chris Dean took immediately to ice dancing, eschewing the figures and formalities of the more orthodox discipline. While Jayne at 14 became national pairs champion, again with Michael Hutchinson, Chris, at the age of 13, won the 1972 British primary ice dance championship. Two years later, he also moved on to win the junior title. But just as Michael Hutchinson moved to London in search of another partner, after he and Jayne Torvill had lost their national title, so Dean split up with his own partner, Sandra Elsom.

In 1975 the accomplished and versatile skater Janet Sawbridge brought Dean and Torvill together. By that time, Chris was a police cadet. Janet Sawbridge, who had not long turned professional, became Nottingham ice rink coach, Dean and Sandra quarreled for the last time, and it was Janet's idea that Dean should skate with Torvill. It has proved to be an inspired match.

Torvill stands only half-an-inch over five feet, and while this makes her an ideal partner for lifts, and the various other acrobatic feats which she and Dean perform on the ice, there was a potentially alarming disparity of 10 inches between them.

They did not make an auspicious beginning. Dancing together on the Nottingham rink for the first time, Torvill fell painfully on her head and elbow. A friend of hers even told Dean that she would never make a good enough partner for him. But they persevered and, coached later by Betty Callaway, things steadily, then dramatically, improved.

It was characteristic of Torvill, that first evening, that she should get up from the ice without complaint. Pain, injury and the need to triumph with mind over matter has often been their lot. Thus when, in March 1983, the two of them won the world title in Helsinki, for the third successive time, it was a tribute to Torvill's fortitude. She had twice fallen painfully in practice—

falls which prevented them competing to retain their European title in Dortmund—and before each performance she now had to have her back and shoulder strapped. The unstrapping afterwards was even more of an ordeal. Meanwhile, Dean was having treatment twice a day for fluid on the knee, and lived under the fear that it might not stand up to the strain.

Of great help to them in Helsinki was Michael Crawford, the ebullient actor and comedian who had played the lead in the musical of *Barnum*, from which they had derived the inspiration for their remarkable new performance.

Assessing their new Olympic routine, Robin Cousins has eulogized the mechanics of their lifts. He praised, particularly, 'a lift two-and-a-half minutes into their free skating routine, over so quickly that it will generally go unnoticed. He lifts her one handed by the bottom of the boot, like a pairs skater. But he puts her in a position she would normally never expect to go to. It probably took them weeks to figure that move out.'

Doubtless it did, for Dean and Torvill are embattled perfectionists, who would rather lose an Olympic title with a remarkable new routine than capture it with one they have already used and mastered.

To see Dean and Torvill on the ice is to see not only a spectacular demonstration of grace, fluency and invention, a sustained defiance of risk and gravity, but a kind of contempt for the banal. For them, the Olympic motto of *citius, altius, fortius*—faster, higher, stronger— seems to have special significance.

They are their own choreographers, their own most implacable and ruthless critics, driving themselves on to greater and greater possibilities. They have taken the art of ice dancing far out of its accustomed range, into an air where it is hard to breathe, or follow them.

Their Olympic victory in Sarajevo was a triumph.

CECILIA COLLEDGE
Figure skating silver, 1936

Should the silver medal for figure skating which the graceful, gifted Cecilia Colledge won in the 1936 Winter Olympics at Garmisch-Partenkirchen really have been a gold? Was the then 15-year-old English girl unfairly graded second to Norway's Sonja Henie, before the latter began her successful Hollywood career? World War II robbed Miss Colledge of another chance.

The daughter of a successful consultant who seldom watched her skate, and a mother who watched her all the time, Miss Colledge began skating as a five-year-old, and actually came eighth in the world and Olympic competitions of 1932 at the phenomenal age of 11.

In Garmisch, Sonja Henie burst into tears on the first day of competition, when Cecilia seemed on the point of overtaking her. 'She will always be a heroine to me,' said Cecilia, that evening, 'whether I beat her or not, and it was her father who first urged Mummy to have me trained as an eventual champion.'

Privately tutored so that she could skate when she pleased, and coached by Jacques Gerschweiler, the tall, slender, blonde Miss Colledge failed next day to wipe out the narrow lead Sonja Henie had established.

After winning her sixth consecutive British title in 1946, she turned professional, went to the United States, and coached at the Boston Skating Club.

JEANETTE ALTWEG

Figure skating gold, 1952

Jeanette Altwegg was one of the last of the simon-pure, exemplary, Olympic skating champions. Sonja Henie had set the pattern 16 years before Jeanette won the figure skating gold in Oslo. Sonja had then turned professional, become a film star, and made a fortune. Jeanette, by utter contrast, turned down all offers to become a professional, and went off to work in the Pestalozzi children's village for wartime orphans at Trogen, in Switzerland.

A fine all-round athlete with a flair for compulsory figures and an admirable temperament, Jeanette was also a finalist in the Junior Wimbledon tennis tournament of 1947, and even gained an air pilot's licence.

In addition to her four British championships, she twice won the European and once the world championship—the latter when she was 21, the year before her Olympic title.

Olympic medallists Cecilia Colledge (left) and Jeanette Altwegg (right) were both figure-skaters of superlative grace.

JOHN CURRY

Figure skating gold, 1976

John Curry's phenomenal achievements as a figure skater, his world, Olympic and European titles, were tributes as much to his strength of will as to his dazzling originality, his capacity to give men's skating a wholly new dimension.

Curry's love of skating began at the age of seven. When he was 16 years old he went to London to be coached at Richmond under the illustrious Swiss, Arnold Gerschweiler. But there was a conflict of what might be called skating philosophy. 'I felt that he had everything he needed to be a champion.' Gerschweiler recalled, 'and I thought I saw the way to translate that ability into reality. But John, being young, saw it a different way.'

Being young? Or merely being precociously wise, instinctively aware and sure of what must be his way? It was in every way a hard time for Curry, privation exacerbated by his battles first with Gerschweiler, then with his subsequent coach at Richmond, Alison Smith. He was obliged to get up at the crack of dawn to find space on the rink, and he was doing a dreary receptionist's job which netted him a mere £13 a week, all but 50 pence a week of which was consumed by what he had to pay for his skating.

What he needed, clearly, was some kind of a Fairy Godfather, and he was lucky enough to find one in the shape of a wealthy American, Ed Moser, who approached him at the 1973 European Championships in Bratislava, and offered his help. A manufacturer of safes for banks and offices, Moser, with his largesse, saw to it that Curry would no longer be the weary, overworked, depressed individual he had been in London, subjected to extra tension by the coaches' opposition to his original approach to the sport.

Now Curry could go where he wished to find a coach: he went to America, and to Italians there. First, it was to Gus Lussi, in Lake Placid, and after that to Carlo Fassi, in Denver. Like Gerschweiler, Fassi at once discerned Curry's huge possibilities. 'The big change,' he said, after coaching him for a while, 'has not been technical: he has always been a very good skater. It has been rather that he never believed in himself. He needed someone to convince him that big things would go right if only he would stop little things bothering him.' Curry also resorted to one of those positive thinking courses so much in vogue in America.

As time passed, Curry became slightly less radical in his approach. In 1976, the vital Olympic year, he modified his programme, clearly aware that skating's judges, with their orthodox background and approach, would not readily be stampeded into so novel a conception of their sport. In 1975, he admitted, 'I was concentrating on skating as beautiful a programme as possible, and the jumps would be incidental to the choreography. But now I realise that this is not what the judges were looking for, and that there are rules. So now the jumps are placed to be the most important part of the programme. And I'm really enjoying myself.

The measure of his victory in Innsbruck in 1976 can be gauged from the fact that no British skater in this event had ever won so much as a medal, and that the best place until then had been in 1908 when, in the London Games, John Kieller Grieg of Scotland finished fourth.

It was Curry's third splendid victory in successive months. Robin Cousins, who finished tenth in Innsbruck, had given Curry a hard fight for the British Championship; then Curry went on to defeat the European champion in January.

Curry, in his victory, was not as spectacular, for example, as the American, Terry Kubicka, who brought off an amazing backward somersault, which had never until then been seen in a championship. But Curry's calm elegance was unbeatable. 'I've enjoyed it very much,' he said afterwards, 'I didn't think I would, to be honest. I thought I was going to have to hide in my room all day. But it's been very exciting. The perfect end to my amateur career'.

ROBIN COUSINS

Figure skating gold, 1980

After the inspired brilliance of John Curry, the controversial new dimension he had given to men's ice skating, and the Olympic, World and European titles he had won, it might have seemed foolish to expect an instant and coruscating successor. But one was at hand. One who, in his way, was every bit as remarkable as Curry, who would retain the gold medal for Britain in the winter Olympics, and who would follow Curry into show business.

Robin Cousins' skating career began one summer day in 1967 in Bournemouth. Rain forced the family off the beach, and chance took them past the ice palace, where photographs of the ice show caught Robin's eye. He was hooked. His Christmas present was half-a-dozen 20-minute lessons at eight shillings a time with the competent Pamela Davies, at Bristol ice rink.

Cousins, from the first, was much more interested in the joys and challenges of free skating than in the formalities of figures; a proclivity that ran right the way through not only to the 1980 Olympics but to the World Championships in Dortmund that followed them.

There, Cousins was forced into second place by his East German rival—who then went back to being a medical student, while Curry plunged into show business. But such was the effervescence of his marvellous free skating programme that it took five *mädchen*, rather than the usual one, to bring him his bouquets.

Pamela Davies continued to coach him, subsequently bringing him up to London once a week, where he received further tuition from the distinguished teacher Gladys Hogg. He skated for his country in the European Championships of 1973, and four years later made the long trip to Denver, to be coached by the explosive Carlo Fussi on his barn-like rink . . . Fussi, who at one championship called him a coward to spur him to greater efforts and ultimate success.

All this cost a good deal of money, and the family rallied round splendidly, Cousins' mother going out to take a job as secretary in a Bristol building firm, and his brother doing a news-

114

paper round. John moved to London and lived in a bleak bedsitting room in Notting Hill Gate. But the whole enterprise would have been impossible without the generous financial help of James Miller, a Scottish builder whose wife, the former international skater Iris Lloyd-Webb, spotted Cousins' gifts.

Three times runner-up to Curry in the British championships, Cousins' approach was altogether more athletic and dashing. 'I love a crowd,' he said, 'and I can respond to them, because without that, there is no inspiration. I love the chance to show off, and give something to somebody.' Show business lay inevitably ahead.

Yet for all his excellence, the Olympic title which he took at Lake Placid in 1980 was a dramatically close-run thing. There were three major rivals, two from the United States, Charles Tickner and David Santee, and one from East Germany, Jan Hoffman. The East German, as expected, was ahead after the short programme, but by so tiny a margin that Cousins could reasonably be expected to leave him behind in his speciality, the free skating.

In this, he was drawn to skate first. 'He wants to go out there first,' said his father, 'and produce the performance of his life, and challenge anyone else to match it.' It was clearly going to be a very hard fight.

And so it was, Cousins prevailing at the last by 0.24 of a point over the East German, after the fright of an early error. Even Cousins admitted, 'I will have to do much better in the World Championships at Dortmund if I am to prove I am worthy champion,' although while acknowledging Hoffman's superiority in the jumps, he insisted that there was a great deal more to free skating than that. 'You should,' he said, 'devise a programme that would still be interesting, even if you took out the jumps, and that is what I try to do.'

THE CHALLENGERS

biographical details

Steve Ovett
(Athletics: middle distance running)
Born 9th October 1955
From Brighton, Sussex
Member Phoenix Athletic Club of Brighton
Olympic 800m champion and 1,500m bronze medallist in Moscow 1980

Steve Cram
(Athletics: middle distance running)
Born 14th October 1960
From Hebburn-on-Tyne, County Durham
Member Jarrow Athletic Club
European junior 3,000m champion 1979
Olympic Games finalist 1,500m 1980
European senior 1,500m champion 1982
Commonwealth Games 1,500m champion 1982
World 1,500m champion 1983

Sebastian Coe
(Athletics: middle distance running)
Born 29th September 1956
From Sheffield, Yorks
Member Haringey Athletic Club
Olympic 1,500m champion and 800m silver medallist, Moscow 1980
Runner-up 800m European Championships 1982

Allan Wells
(Athletics: sprints)
Born 3rd May 1952
From Edinburgh, Scotland
Member Edinburgh Southern Harriers
Commonwealth Games 100m and 200m champion
Olympic 100m champion and 200m silver medallist, Moscow 1980

Daley Thompson
(Athletics: decathlon)
Born 30th July 1958
From Crawley, Sussex
Member Newham & Essex Beagles Athletic Club
European, Commonwealth, World and Olympic decathlon champion

Judy Livermore
(Athletics: heptathlon)
Born 14th November 1960
From Nuneaton, Warwickshire
Member Birchfield Harriers
Competed in the pentathlon at the 1980 Olympic Games in Moscow
Runner-up in the heptathlon at the Commonwealth Games in Brisbane 1982 and third in the World Student Games in Edmonton 1983

Fatima Whitbread
(Athletics: javelin)
Born 3rd March 1961
From Grays, Essex
Member Thurrock Athletic Club
European junior champion 1979
Competed in the Commonwealth Games in Edmonton 1978 and Brisbane 1982
Runner-up World Championships, Helsinki 1983

Neil Adams
(Judo)
Born 27th September 1958
From Rugby, Warwickshire
Member Budokwai Club
Olympic Games silver medallist 1980
European junior champion 1974, 1977
European senior champion 1979, 1980, 1983
World Champion 1981
Runner-up World Championship 1983

Andrew Morris
(Gymnastics)
Born 30th November 1961
From Swansea, Glamorgan
Member City of Swansea Gymnastics Club
British National overall champion
Highest scoring West European male gymnast in 1983 European Championships

Lucinda Green
(Equestrian events)
Born 7th November 1953
From Andover, Hants
European three-day event champion 1975, 1977; runner-up 1983
British Olympic team Montreal 1976
World three-day event champion

Beryl Mitchell
(Rowing)
Born 26th June 1950
Lives and teaches in West London
Member Thames Tradesmen Rowing Club
Competed in Olympic Games in Montreal 1976 (coxless pair) and in Moscow 1980 (single sculls)
Fifth place in Olympic final 1980
Runner-up in World Championship 1981 (single sculls)

Chris Snode
(Diving: springboard and highboard)
Born 23rd March 1959
From Romford, Essex
Member Highgate Diving Club
European springboard champion
Commonwealth Games highboard and springboard champion 1978 and 1982
Sixth in the springboard diving competition at the 1980 Olympic Games

Phil Hubble
(Swimming: butterfly)
Born 19th July 1960
From Slough, Berks
Member Hounslow Swimming Club
Runner-up 200m butterfly Olympic Games 1980
Commonwealth Games champion 200m butterfly
Also runner-up 100m butterfly, 4 x 100 medley relay
4 x 100 and 4 x 200 freestyle relays Commonwealth Games Brisbane 1982
Runner-up 200m butterfly World Student Games, Edmonton 1983

Adrian Moorhouse
(Swimming: breaststroke)
Born 24th May 1964
From Leeds, Yorks.
Member Leeds Central Swimming Club
European 200m breaststroke champion
Commonwealth Games 100m breaststroke champion
Also runner-up 4 x 100m medley relay and third 200m breaststroke 1982 Commonwealth Games

Jayne Torvill and Christopher Dean
(Ice dancing)
Born– Jayne: 7th October 1957; Chris: 27th July 1958
Both from Nottingham, Notts
Members Nottingham Ice Dance and Figure Skating Club
European champions 1981, 1982, 1984
World champions 1981, 1982, 1983
Awarded Freedom of the City of Nottingham 1983
Olympic champions 1984. They won their Olympic title at the Winter Games in Sarajevo in February of this year and have since turned professional.

THE PAINTINGS

Oil on Canvas

Page		
2	Olympic Torch and Arm	37" x 19"
6-7	Olympic Triptych	72" x 180"
11	Olympic Flag and Flame	30" x 22"
13	Steve Ovett	17" x 17"
17	Steve Cram	36" x 29"
21	Sebastian Coe	16" x 14"
35	Allan Wells	30" x 23"
43	Daley Thompson	54" x 44"
47	Judy Livermore	40" x 30"
49	Javelin	36" x 14"
51	Fatima Whitbread	36" x 24"
65	Neil Adams	48" x 36"
67	Injured Gymnast	36" x 24"
69	Andrew Morris	50" x 48"
71	Lucinda Green	66" x 30"
73	Parthenon Horse, British Museum	12" x 16"
75	Beryl Mitchell	46" x 36"
77	Divers' Dance	84" x 60"
79	Chris Snode	60" x 54"
83	Phil Hubble	40" x 30"
107	Torvill and Dean	42" x 60"

Watercolours — All 40" x 30"

33	Allan Wells	
76	Beryl Mitchell	
81	Diver through portholes	
85	Adrian Moorhouse	
89	Adrian Moorhouse	
95	Cathy White	
103	Nigel Standish	
104	Diver	
105	Reflections – Olympic thoughts	

Drawings — Both 40" x 30"

48	Judy Livermore	
66	Neil Adams	

PHOTOGRAPH CREDITS

Allsport Photographic
pages 24, 25, 28, 38, 51

BBC Hulton Picture Library
pages 26, 41, 88, 100, 110, 113

Tony Duffy/Allsport Photographic
pages 61, 96, 97, 99, 114

Keystone Press Agency
pages 27, 29, 31, 32, 52, 54, 55, 59, 72, 94, 98, 102, 111

Popperfoto
pages 53, 58, 91, 92, 115

S & G Press Agency Limited
pages 63, 93

Syndication International Limited
pages 40, 57

Topham Picture Library
pages 89, 90

MAJOR BRITISH TRIUMPHS SINCE 1896

1896 Athens
Cycling: individual road race *bronze* — F. Battel
Tennis: men's singles *gold* — John Boland
Weightlifting: heavyweight (one-hand lift) *gold* — Launceston Eliot
    (two-hand lift) *silver* — Launceston Eliot

1900 Paris
Rowing: single sculls *bronze* — St George Ashe
Swimming: 1,000 metres freestyle *gold* — John Jarvis
    4,000 metres freestyle *gold* — John Jarvis
    obstacle event 200 metres *bronze* — Peter Kemp
Tennis: men's singles *gold* — Hugh Doherty
    silver — Harold Mahoney
    bronze — Reginald Doherty
    bronze — A.B. Norris
    women's singles *gold* — Charlotte Cooper
    men's doubles *gold* — Reginald Doherty, Hugh Doherty
    mixed doubles *gold* — Charlotte Cooper, Reginald Doherty
Track & field: high jump *silver* — Patrick Leahy
    800 metres *gold* — Alfred Tysoe
    1,500 metres *gold* — Charles Bennett
    4,000 metres steeplechase *gold* — John Rimmer
    4,000 metres steeplechase *silver* — Charles Bennett
    4,000 metres steeplechase *bronze* — Sidney Robinson
    2,500 metres steeplechase *silver* — Sidney Robinson
    5,000 metres team race *gold* — Great Britain
Yachting: open class *gold* — Great Britain
    ½–1 ton class *gold* — Great Britain
    2–3 ton class *gold* — Great Britain
    3–10 ton class *bronze* — (shared with France) Great Britain
    10–20 ton class *bronze* — Great Britain

1904 St Louis
Track & field: 4,000 metres steeplechase *silver* — John Daly

1906 Athens
Cycling: 1,000 metres sprint *silver* — H.C. Bouffler
    2,000 metres tandem *gold* — J. Matthews, A. Rushen
    20,000 metres track *gold* — William Pett
Shooting: Olympic trap shooting (single shot) *gold* — Gerald Merlin
    bronze — Sidney Merlin
    (double shot) *gold* — Sidney Merlin
    bronze — Gerald Merlin
Swimming: 1,000 metres freestyle *gold* — Henry Taylor
    silver — John Jarvis
    400 metres freestyle *silver* — Henry Taylor
    bronze — John Jarvis
Track & field: high jump *gold* — Con Leahy
    long jump *gold* — Peter O'Connor
    400 metres *silver* — Wyndham Halswelle
    800 metres *bronze* — Wyndham Halswelle
    1,500 metres *silver* — John McGough
    10,000 metres *gold* — Henry Hawtrey
    110 metres hurdles *silver* — A.H. Healey

1908 London
Archery: York round *gold* — William Dod
    silver — R.P. Brooks King
Boxing: bantamweight *gold* — Henry Thomas
    silver — John Condon
    bronze — W. Webb
    featherweight *gold* — Richard Gunn
    silver — C.W. Morris
    bronze — Hugh Roddin
    lightweight *gold* — Frederick Grace
    silver — Frederick Spiller
    bronze — H.H. Johnson
    middleweight *gold* — John Douglas
    bronze — W. Philo
    heavyweight *gold* — A.L. Oldham
    silver — S.C.H. Evans
    bronze — Frederick Parks
Cycling: 2,000 metres tandem *silver* — F.G. Hamlin, H. Thomas Johnson
    bronze — Colin Brooks, Walter Isaacs
    5,000 metres track *gold* — Benjamin Jones
    20,000 metres track *gold* — Charles Kingsbury
    100 kilometres track *gold* — Charles Bartlett
    silver — Charles Denny
    600 yards *gold* — Victor Johnson
Figure skating: men's *silver* — Arthur Cumming
    men's *bronze* — George Hall-Say
    pair's *silver* — Phyllis Johnson, James Johnson
    bronze —
    women's *gold* — Madge Syers

1908 London – continued
Polo *gold* — Great Britain
    silver — Great Britain
    bronze — Great Britain
Rackets: singles *gold* — Evan Noel
    silver — Henry Leaf
    bronze — John Jacob Astor
    doubles *silver* — Edward Bury, Cecil Browning
    bronze — Evan Noel, Henry Leaf
Rowing: coxless pairs *gold* — J.R.K. Fenning, Gordon Thomson
    silver — George Fairbairn, Philip Verdon
    single sculls *gold* — Harry Blackstaffe
    silver — Alexander McCulloch
Rugby Union *silver* — Great Britain
    bronze — Great Britain
Shooting: free rifle *gold* — Jerry Milner
    bronze — Maurice Blood
    Olympic trap shooting *bronze* — Alexander Maunder
    running deer shooting (single shot) *bronze* — A.E. Rogers
    silver — Ted Ranken
    (double shot) *silver* — Ted Ranken
    small-bore rifle *gold* — A.A. Carnell
    silver — Harry Humby
    bronze — G. Barnes
    (disappearing target) *gold* — William Styles
    silver — H.I. Hawkins
    bronze — E.J. Amoore
    (moving target) *gold* — A.F. Fleming
    silver — M.K. Matthews
Swimming: 200 metres breaststroke *gold* — Frederick Holman
    silver — William Robinson
    400 metres freestyle *gold* — Henry Taylor
    1,500 metres freestyle *gold* — Henry Taylor
    silver — Sydney Battersby
Tennis: men's singles *gold* — Josiah Ritchie
    bronze — Wilberforce Eves
    (indoor) *gold* — Wentworth Gore
    bronze — Josiah Ritchie
    men's doubles *gold* — George Hillyard, Reginald Doherty
    silver — Josiah Ritchie, James Parke
    bronze — Charles Cazalet, Charles Dixon
    (indoor) *gold* — Wentworth Gore, Herbert Barrett
    silver — George Simond, George Caridia
    women's singles *gold* — Dorothea Chambers
    silver — Dorothea Boothby
    bronze — Joan Winch
    (indoor) *gold* — Gwen Eastlake-Smith
    silver — Angela Greene
Track & field: high jump *silver* — Con Leahy
    400 metres hurdles *bronze* — Leonard Tremeer
    400 metres *gold* — Wyndham Halswelle
    1,500 metres *silver* — Harold Wilson
    bronze — Norman Hallows
    10,000 metres *gold* — Emil Voigt
    silver — Edward Owen
    shot put *silver* — Dennis Horgan
Track & field: 3,000 metres steeplechase *gold* — Arthur Russell
    silver — Archie Robertson
    3 miles team race *gold* — Great Britain
    triple jump *gold* — Tim Ahearne
    3,500 metres walk *gold* — George Larner
    silver — Ernest Webb
    10 miles walk *gold* — George Larner
    silver — Ernest Webb
    bronze — Edward Spencer
Water polo *gold* — Great Britain
Wrestling: free-style (bantamweight) *silver* — William Press
    (lightweight) *silver* — William Wood
    (middleweight) *gold* — Stanley Bacon
    silver — George de Relwyskow
    bronze — Frederick Beck
    (heavyweight) *gold* — George O'Kelly
    bronze — Edmond Barrett
Yachting: 6 metres class *gold* — Great Britain
    7 metres class *gold* — Great Britain
    8 metres class *gold* — Great Britain
    12 metres class *bronze* — Great Britain
    12 metres class *gold* — Great Britain
    silver — Great Britain

1912 Stockholm
Cycling: individual road race *silver* — Frederick Grubb
Rowing: single sculls *silver* — Jack Beresford
Shooting: free pistol (50 metres) *bronze* — Charles Stewart
    small-bore rifle *silver* — William Milne
    bronze — Harry Burt
Swimming: women's highboard diving *bronze* — Isabelle White
    100 metres freestyle *bronze* — Jennie Fletcher
    400 metres freestyle *silver* — John Hatfield
    1,500 metres freestyle *silver* — John Hatfield
    4 x 100 metres relay *gold* — Great Britain
    obstacle event (200 metres) *bronze* — Percy Courtman
Tennis: men's singles (indoor) *silver* — Charles Dixon
    men's doubles (indoor) *bronze* — Charles Dixon, Arthur Beamish
    mixed doubles (indoor) *gold* — Ethel Hannam, Charles Dixon
    silver — Helen Aitchison, Herbert Barrett
    women's singles (indoor) *gold* — Ethel Hannam
    bronze — Mabel Parton
Water Polo *gold* — Great Britain
Track & field: cross country (team) *bronze* — Great Britain
    200 metres *gold* — Ralph Craig
    bronze — Willie Applegarth
    1,500 metres *gold* — Arnold Jackson
    5,000 metres *bronze* — George Hutson
    4 x 100 metres relay *gold* — Great Britain
    4 x 400 metres relay *bronze* — Great Britain
    10,000 metres walk *silver* — Ernest Webb

1920 Antwerp
Boxing: flyweight *bronze* — William Cuthbertson
    bantamweight *bronze* — James McKenzie
    welterweight *silver* — Alexander Ireland
    middleweight *gold* — Harry Mallin
    light heavyweight *bronze* — H. Franks
Cycling: 1,000 metres sprint *silver* — H. Thomas Johnson
    bronze — Harry Ryan
    2,000 metres tandem *gold* — Harry Ryan, Thomas Lance
    50,000 metres track *silver* — Cyril Alden
Figure skating: pairs *bronze* — Basil Williams, Phyllis Johnson
Rugby Union *bronze* — Great Britain
Swimming: women's highboard diving *silver* — Eileen Armstrong
    4 x 100 metres freestyle relay *silver* — Great Britain
Tennis: men's singles *bronze* — Charles Winslow
    men's doubles *gold* — Noel Turnbull, Max Woosnam
    mixed doubles *silver* — Kitty McKane, Max Woosnam
    women's singles *silver* — Dorothy Holman
    women's doubles *gold* — Winifred McNair, Kitty McKane
    silver — Gerald Beamish, Dorothy Holman
Track & field: 100 metres *bronze* — Harry Edward
    200 metres *bronze* — Harry Edward
    400 metres *silver* — Guy Butler
    800 metres *gold* — Albert Hill
    1,500 metres *gold* — Albert Hill
    silver — Philip Baker
    10,000 metres *bronze* — James Wilson
    3,000 metres steeplechase *gold* — Percy Hodge
    4 x 400 metres relay *gold* — Great Britain
    3,000 metres team race *silver* — Great Britain
    Team cross country *silver* — Great Britain
    10,000 metres walk *bronze* — Charles Gunn

1924 Paris (*Winter:* Chamonix/Mont Blanc)
Bobsledding: 4-man bob *silver* — Great Britain
Boxing: flyweight *silver* — James McKenzie
    middleweight *gold* — Harry Mallin
    silver — John Elliott
    light heavyweight *gold* — Harry Mitchell
Cycling: 50,000 metres track *silver* — Cyril Alden
    bronze — Frederick Wyld
Fencing: women's foil (individual) *silver* — Gladys Davis
Figure skating: women's *bronze* — Ethel Muckelt
Ice hockey *bronze* — Great Britain
Polo *bronze* — Great Britain
Rowing: single sculls *gold* — Jack Beresford
Shooting: running deer shooting (single shot) *silver* — C.W. Mackworth-Praed
    (double shot) *silver* — C.W. Mackworth-Praed
Swimming: 100 metres backstroke *silver* — Phyllis Harding
    200 metres breaststroke *gold* — Lucy Morton
    bronze — Gladys Carson
    4 x 100 metres freestyle relay *silver* — Great Britain
    plain high diving *bronze* — Harold Clarke
Tennis: women's singles *bronze* — Kitty McKane
    women's doubles *silver* — Edith Covell, Kitty McKane
    bronze — Dorothy Shepherd-Barron, Evelyn Colyer

1924 (continued)
Track & field: hammer *bronze* — Malcolm Nokes
    100 metres *gold* — Harold Abrahams
    200 metres *bronze* — Eric Liddell
    400 metres *gold* — Eric Liddell
    800 metres *gold* — Douglas Lowe
    1,500 metres *bronze* — Henry Stallard
    4 x 400 metres relay *bronze* — Great Britain
    4 x 100 metres relay *silver* — Great Britain
    3,000 metres team race *silver* — Great Britain
    10,000 metres walk *silver* — Gordon Goodwin
Wrestling: free-style (heavyweight) *bronze* — Andrew McDonald
Yachting: 8 metres class *silver* — Great Britain

1928 Amsterdam (*Winter:* St Moritz)
Cycling: 2,000 metres tandem *silver* — John Sibbit, Ernest Chambers
    individual road race *silver* — Frank Southall
Fencing: women's foil (individual) *silver* — Muriel Freeman
Rowing: coxless pairs *silver* — Archibald Nisbet, Terence O'Brien
    single sculls *bronze* — David Collet
Swimming: 100 metres backstroke *bronze* — Joyce Cooper
    4 x 100 metres freestyle relay *silver* — Great Britain
Tobogganing: skeleton sled *bronze* — Earl of Northesk
Track & field: 400 metres hurdles *gold* — Lord Burghley
    100 metres *silver* — Jack London
    200 metres *silver* — Walter Rangeley
    800 metres *gold* — Douglas Lowe
    4 x 100 metres relay *bronze* — Great Britain
Wrestling: free-style (middleweight) *bronze* — Samuel Rabin

1932 Los Angeles (*Winter:* Lake Placid)
Cycling: 2,000 metres tandem *silver* — Ernest Chambers, Stanley Chambers
Fencing: women's foil (individual) *silver* — Heather Guinness
Rowing: coxless pairs *gold* — Arthur Edwards, Lewis Clive
Swimming: 4 x 100 metres freestyle relay *bronze* — Great Britain
Track & field: 110 metres hurdles *gold* — George Sailing
    bronze — Don Finlay
    marathon *silver* — Sam Ferris
    800 metres *gold* — Thomas Hampson
    1,500 metres *silver* — John Cornes
    4 x 400 metres women's relay *silver* — Great Britain
    4 x 100 metres women's relay *silver* — Great Britain
    50,000 metres road walk *gold* — Thomas Green
    3,000 metres steeplechase *silver* — Tom Evenson

1936 Berlin (*Winter:* Garmisch-Partenkirchen)
Bobsledding: 4-man bob *bronze* — Great Britain
Figure skating: women's *silver* — Cecilia Colledge
Ice hockey *gold* — Great Britain
Track & field: women's high jump *silver* — Dorothy Odam
    110 metres hurdles *silver* — Don Finlay
    400 metres *silver* — Godfrey Brown
    4 x 100 metres women's relay *silver* — Great Britain
    4 x 400 metres relay *gold* — Great Britain
    50,000 metres road walk *gold* — Harold Whitlock
    marathon *silver* — Ernest Harper
Yachting: International Star class *silver* — Great Britain
    6 metres class *gold* — Great Britain

1948 London (*Winter:* St Moritz)
Boxing: middleweight *silver* — John Wright
    light heavyweight *silver* — Donald Scott
Cycling: 1,000 metres time-trial *bronze* — Thomas Godwin
    2,000 metres tandem *silver* — Reg Harris, Alan Bannister
Figure skating: women's *bronze* — Jeanette Altwegg
Rowing: coxless pairs *gold* — John Wilson, William Laurie
    double sculls *gold* — Herbert Bushnell, Richard D. Burnell
Swimming: 400 metres freestyle *bronze* — Cathy Gibson
Tobogganing: skeleton sled *bronze* — John Crammond
Track & field: women's high jump *silver* — Dorothy Tyler
    women's 100 metres *silver* — Dorothy Manley
    women's 200 metres *silver* — Audrey Williamson
Track & field: 4 x 100 metres relay *silver* — Great Britain
    50,000 metres road walk *bronze* — Tebbs Lloyd Johnson
Weightlifting: lightweight *bronze* — James Halliday
Yachting: Swallow class *gold* — Stewart Morris, David Bond

119

1952 Helsinki *(Winter:* Oslo)
Equestrian: grand prix (jumping) team *gold* — Great Britain
Figure skating: women's *gold* — Jeanette Altwegg
Swimming: 200 metres breaststroke *bronze* — Helen Gordon
Track & field: women's high jump *silver* — Sheila Lerwill
women's long jump *bronze* — Shirley Cawley
100 metres *bronze* — Emmanuel M.C.D. Bailey
women's 4 x 100 metres relay *bronze* — Great Britain
3,000 metres steeplechase *bronze* — John Disley
Wrestling: free-style (heavyweight) *bronze* — Kenneth Richmond
Yachting: Olympic monotype class *silver* — Charles Currey

1956 Melbourne/Stockholm *(Winter:* Cortina d'Ampezzo)
Boxing: flyweight *gold* — Terence Spinks
featherweight *silver* — Thomas Nicholls
lightweight *gold* — Richard McTaggart
welterweight *bronze* — Nicholas Gargano
light middleweight *bronze* (shared) — John McCormack
Cycling: individual road race *bronze* — Alan Jackson
Equestrian: 3-day event *bronze* — Frank Weldon
Fencing: women's foil (individual) *gold* — Gillian Sheen
Swimming: 100 metres backstroke *gold* — Judy Grinham
bronze — Margaret Edwards
Track & field: women's high jump *silver* — Thelma Hopkins
800 metres *silver* — Derek Johnson
5,000 metres *silver* — Gordon Pirie
bronze — Derek Ibbotson
4 x 400 metres relay *bronze* — Great Britain
women's 4 x 400 metres relay *silver* — Great Britain
3,000 metres steeplechase *gold* — Chris Brasher
Yachting: Dragon class *bronze* — Great Britain
Flying Dutchman class *bronze* — Great Britain
5.5 metres class *silver* — Great Britain

1960 Rome *(Winter:* Squaw Valley)
Boxing: lightweight *bronze* — Richard McTaggart
welterweight *bronze* — James Lloyd
light middleweight *bronze* — William Asher
Equestrian: grand prix (jumping) *bronze* — David Broome
Fencing: épée individual *silver* — Alan Jay
Swimming: 100 metres backstroke *silver* — Natalie Steward
200 metres breaststroke *gold* — Anita Lonsbrough
high board diving *bronze* — Brian Phelps
100 metres freestyle *bronze* — Natalie Steward
women's springboard diving *bronze* — Elizabeth Ferris
Track & field: women's 100 metres hurdles *silver* — Carol Quinton
100 metres *bronze* — Peter Radford
women's 100 metres *bronze* — Dorothy Hyman
women's 200 metres *bronze* — Dorothy Hyman
4 x 100 metres relay *bronze* — Great Britain
20,000 metres road walk *bronze* — Stan Vickers
50,000 metres road walk *gold* — Don Thompson
Weightlifting: middle-heavyweight *bronze* — Louis Martin

1964 Tokyo *(Winter:* Innsbruck)
Bobsledding: 2-man bob *gold* — Tony Nash, Robin Dixon
Equestrian: grand prix (jumping) *bronze* — Peter Robeson
Fencing: épée individual *silver* — William Hoskyns
Swimming: 100 metres freestyle *silver* — Bobbie McGregor
Track & field: 400 metres hurdles *silver* — John Cooper
long jump *gold* — Lynn Davies
women's long jump *gold* — Mary Rand
women's 400 metres *silver* — Ann Packer
women's 800 metres *gold* — Ann Packer
women's pentathlon *silver* — Mary Rand
marathon *silver* — Basil Heatley
4 x 400 metres relay *silver* — Great Britain
women's 4 x 400 metres relay *bronze* — Great Britain
20,000 metres road walk *gold* — Ken Matthews
50,000 metres road walk *silver* — Paul Nihill
3,000 metres steeplechase *silver* — Maurice Herriot
Weightlifting: middle-heavyweight *silver* — Louis Martin
Yachting: Flying Dutchman class *silver* — Keith Musto, Arthur Morgan

1968 Mexico City *(Winter:* Grenoble)
Boxing: middleweight *gold* — Christopher Finnegan
Equestrian: grand prix (jumping) *silver* — Marion Coates
bronze — David Broome
3-day event *silver* — Derek Allhusen
Swimming: 200 metres butterfly *silver* — Martyn Woodruff
Track & field: 400 metres hurdles *gold* — David Hemery
bronze — John Sherwood
women's long jump *silver* — Sheila Sherwood
women's 400 metres *silver* — Lilian Board
Yachting: Flying Dutchman class *gold* — Rodney Pattisson, I. MacDonald-Smith
5.5 metres class *bronze* — Great Britain

1972 Munich *(Winter:* Sapporo)
Boxing: bantamweight *bronze* — George Turpin
light middleweight *bronze* — Alan Minter
Equestrian: grand prix (jumping) *silver* — Ann Moore
3-day event *gold* — Richard Meade
Judo: 80kg to 93kg *silver* — David Starbrook
Track & field: 400 metres hurdles *bronze* — David Hemery
4 x 400 metres *bronze* — Great Britain
5,000 metres *bronze* — Ian Stewart
women's pentathlon *gold* — Mary Peters
Yachting: Flying Dutchman class *gold* — Rodney Pattisson, Christopher Davies
International Tempest class *silver* — Alan Warren, David Hunt

1976 Montreal *(Winter:* Innsbruck)
Boxing: bantamweight *bronze* — Patrick Cowdell
Figure skating: men's *gold* — John Curry
Judo: 80kg to 93kg *bronze* — David Starbrook
Track & field: 10,000 metres *bronze* — Brendan Foster
Swimming: 100 metres breaststroke *silver* — David Wilkie
200 metres breaststroke *gold* — David Wilkie
Yachting: International Tornado class *gold* — Great Britain
Flying Dutchman class *silver* — Rodney Pattisson, Julian Brooke Houghton

1980 Moscow *(Winter:* Lake Placid)
Boxing: light-welterweight *bronze* — Anthony Willis
Figure skating: men's *gold* — Robin Cousins
Judo: open *bronze* — Arthur Mapp
up to 71kg *silver* — Neil Adams
Swimming: 100 metres breaststroke *gold* — Duncan Goodhew
200 metres butterfly *silver* — Phil Hubble
400 metres individual medley *silver* — Sharron Davies
4 x 100 metres medley relay *silver* — Great Britain
Track & field: decathlon *gold* — Daley Thompson
400 metres hurdles *bronze* — Gary Oakes
100 metres *gold* — Allan Wells
200 metres *silver* — Allan Wells
800 metres *gold* — Steve Ovett
silver — Sebastian Coe
1,500 metres *gold* — Sebastian Coe
bronze — Steve Ovett
4 x 100 metres relay *bronze* — Great Britain
women's 4 x 400 metres relay *bronze* — Great Britain